EAST ANGLIAN
FOLKLORE
AND
OTHER TALES

Also by W. H. Barrett

Tales from the Fens
More Tales from the Fens
A Fenman's Story

EAST ANGLIAN
FOLKLORE
AND
OTHER TALES

W. H. Barrett
and
R. P. Garrod

PEN AND INK DRAWINGS BY R. P. GARROD

ROUTLEDGE & KEGAN PAUL
London, Henley and Boston

First published in 1976
by Routledge & Kegan Paul Ltd
76 Carter Lane,
London EC4V 5EL,
Reading Road,
Henley-on-Thames,
Oxon RG9 1EN and
9 Park Street,
Boston, Mass. 02108, USA
Set in 11 on 12 pt Monotype Joanna
and printed in Great Britain by
Cox & Wyman Ltd
London, Fakenham and Reading

ISBN 0 7100 8300 9

CONTENTS

Foreword vii

Introduction I by W. H. Barrett ix

Introduction II by R. P. Garrod xi

Obituary xiii

Acknowledgments xv

PART I

EAST ANGLIAN FOLKLORE AND OTHER TALES

Old Job 3

Ratty's Tale 7

By Royal Command 12

Bee Lore 16

Curing Witches 21

The Ghost of Bawburgh Churchyard 27

Melton Ghosts and Others 33

Johnny and Jenny 36

The Game-keeper and his Daughter 40

CONTENTS

Poachers, Convicts, Mantraps   47

St Roch and Rats and Other Things   53

St Winnald's Fair   57

Unkindly Light Lead Thou Me On   60

Mistaken Identity   64

On and Off the Gold Standard   66

Fiddler and Others   71

Darkest East Anglia   74

Walking, Workhouses, Worms   78

A Fen Mystery   85

Edward Rigby   89

Bawburgh's Treasure   91

Stone Coffins Make Fine Pig-feeding Troughs   96

Fertile Seed of Ishmael   99

Old Shuck   103

Beak and Claw Justice   106

Learning the Hard Way   109

PART II

NOTES AND STORIES, TAPE RECORDINGS, FROM DIARY OF VISITS TO W. H. BARRETT

PART III

REST OF THE TALES, GLEANED FROM MATERIAL OBTAINED FROM ANNE BARRETT

Going to Bungay   125

Hospital Patient – 1913 Style   130

PART IV

ANNE BARRETT – LIFE-LONG NURSE

Anne – The Nurse   135

FOREWORD

I feel it a privilege and pleasure to help introduce Mr R. P. Garrod and bring into prominence his integrity and initiative, in his role of co-author of this book, which he has now been able to complete. Owing to fading health, Mr W. H. Barrett, author of *Tales from the Fens* and associated books, was unable to do so.

The friendship sprang from the common interest of writing. Mr Garrod has many accomplishments, such as handicrafts, painting, photography, drawing and writing, and as a result of appropriate use of the latter two achievements he has been able to conclude an interesting book.

I regard this foreword as being, too, a small tribute to Percy Garrod's friendship and to the memory of my late husband, Walter Henry ('Jack') Barrett.

A. A. M. Barrett

INTRODUCTION
I

I was about ten years of age when I first started writing down the tales old men used to tell of bygone days. That was more than seventy years ago [Written 1968 – R.P.G.].

There was no money to spare in those days to buy notebooks but I managed quite well. I used to beg for old wall paper pattern books from the painter and decorator. The local tailor also would give me his out-of-date cloth pattern books. I would tear out the cloth, and paste old auction bills and any other paper I could obtain, in both types of book.

In a very few years I was the possessor of several bulky tomes which contained the cream of local folklore stories; all heard first hand by me.

These books were stored in a cupboard under the stairs. I kept adding to them until 1914, when I was called to an urgent job elsewhere. On my return in 1918, I discovered that as a result of the river bank near our home bursting, the water had flooded this to the depth of several feet and what with this and the waves bursting down the cupboard door, I lost my treasured collection.

W. H. Barrett

INTRODUCTION
II

What W. H. Barrett ('Jack' Barrett nicknamed 'Jack' because in his early years he resembled an uncle of that name) omitted to state in his brief introduction was that his long-term memory plus his tenacity stood him in good stead in spite of that early loss. The 'proof of the pudding' can be seen in both his earlier books and the tales herein recorded.

To have had three books published and joint authorship of another, after reaching seventy-two years of age, was the achievement of 'Jack' Barrett. As a number of folk will know, he was for very many years completely deaf. The only way one could hold conversation with him was to write and for this purpose a notebook was always to hand. In general, lip-reading was not a success, although Mrs Barrett could get many messages across by that medium.

One would have thought that being deaf would tend to make a man bitter. Quite the opposite in this case because an ever-present sense of humour often resulted in 'Jack' telling a tale against himself. Just an example or two he told me and which I put down soon after the telling rather than commit to memory.

Before he was completely deaf and when he was living at Holt and where his wife was the local midwife he would be at hand to answer the telephone when his good lady was out on her rounds.

Their telephone was 3 and occasionally rings were received in mistake. Once when this happened 'Jack' asked the caller whether he wanted the midwife. 'Midwife be B———. I want a plumber.' The call came from a local barracks. The caller required 399 – only one 9 short but the professions poles apart. Of course our story-teller admitted that being even partially deaf was not the best of aids for a person hanging on to one end of a telephone line.

How about this puckish one too, by way of introduction under the heading 'New Contributors' to a story in the *East Anglian Magazine* (March, 1958):

W. H. Barrett was born in Norfolk and has been a gardener most of his life. Estimates he has turned over with a spade thousands of tons of soil in Essex, Suffolk and Norfolk and by virtue of this claims to be a real East Anglian. Education: board school until age of 11, later graduating in the hard school of life. Clubs: Oddfellows and Littlewoods. Hobbies: Drawing my pension and cashing the tobacco coupons. Also interested in the gravitational pull of present-day beer in relation to restricted income. Served during the First World War in the Suffolk Regiment, later transferring to Royal Naval Division. Decorations: two gas-damaged lungs.

What W. H. B. could have mentioned too was that he owed the onset of his deafness to the fact of a comrade in training in that war with him, on one particular occasion pulling out the pin of a hand grenade then failing to part with the grenade with dire results to himself and not too happy results affecting those around him.

Now W. H. himself has passed on and thus what started as far as this book is concerned as a joint effort has been carried on in solo fashion; this being the expressed wish of Mrs Barrett, whose expert nursing – she herself attained her state registration nursing qualifications as long back as 1912 – did undoubtedly postpone the sad finale on 2 November, 1974: with which sentiment I feel certain the other medical friends who were in close touch with him over the years will agree.

R. P. Garrod

OBITUARY

'Barrett – November 2nd. Walter Henry, dearly loved husband of Anne Adela, of Framingham Pigot, affectionate father of Duncan and Joan (deceased), aged 83 years. (Funeral service private.)'

The foregoing notice appearing in a local paper in 1974 brought to an end a long chapter of suffering of the man who once said: 'Having been near to death a number of times right from a youngster, I hold no fear of it now that I'm an old man.'

To me fell the honour and privilege of sharing his actual passing with his wife Anne, at her wish; those moments most sacred to her and which memory will assuredly remain in my memory for all my time.

'Jack' Barrett decreed that he did not want there to be any fuss after his decease; 'do not want to be paraded round the village'; did not want any mourning; did not want any ambiguous floral tributes; hoped those relatives and close friends would partake of the old-time after-funeral tea. His wishes were carried out to the letter and in spirit on the day he was laid to rest in the little churchyard of picturesque Framingham Pigot on Thursday 5 November. Over his grave were laid profuse posies of flowers, simple posies and symbolic of the gardens and their flowers he had loved so well.

To Anne now falls the task, after years of devoted nursing, of picking up the threads again; this now after the loss of all the immediate members of her family. She must know she need not fear, because that task will assuredly be shared by relatives and a close band of friends.

R. P. Garrod

ACKNOWLEDGMENTS

I am grateful to the *East Anglian Magazine* for permission to reproduce 'Curing Witches', this article having previously appeared in *EAM*, March 1958; and the *Eastern Daily Press* for permission to include the article 'Hospital Patient – 1913 Style'.

Thanks too to those good people who, over the years, have satisfied – more often than not – an enquiring mind, with what at the time may have appeared to be isolated and unconnected pieces of information and stories but which used collectively have proved – at least to the writer – in outcome to be even more satisfying and, it is hoped, to be at times useful, too, to other people.

EAST ANGLIAN
FOLKLORE
AND
OTHER TALES

OLD JOB

My first contact with the old man was when I was eight years of age, when, with other boys and girls I was conscripted to work in a gang, of which he was gang master. He would contract with the farmers to supply labour to hoe the corn, pull up docks and thistles; and when the potatoes were lifted he would supply the pickers-up. Besides boys and girls, he would employ women too. He had to have a licence granted by a magistrate to employ the latter, owing to years gone by, a lusty gang master working in a field with healthy buxom women caused grave concern at the number of births of prospective future gang masters. Hence a local by-law was passed that all gang masters must be licensed.

When Job attended the local police court, on being asked his age, his reply was, 'I shall be 85 next birthday, for I was born in 1816 two days after my father was hung at Ely for the part he took in the Littleport riots.' On handing the old man his permit, the magistrate remarked, 'You are the right man for the job, but being a farmer myself, I cannot help thinking that at your age you will be like a bullock in a field with a herd of cows.' Job was proud of this tribute to his impotency. He lost his permit later when one of his gang, a single woman, entered the local work-house where she gave birth to what the Poor Law regulations termed a bastard. On being questioned regarding the father of the child, she replied, 'Old Job.' This did not worry the old chap, for he could turn his hand to any farm work.

He was a strong, healthy man, and also had a very active brain which was a storehouse of folklore down the ages. I used to spend a lot of time in his company listening to his stories of bygone years in Fenland. Just at the time I left school and started work on a farm, Job was given the job to cut down the willows in an osier bed which had been allowed to grow until the stems were over

FENMAN'S LODGE ∾

FRAMEWORK

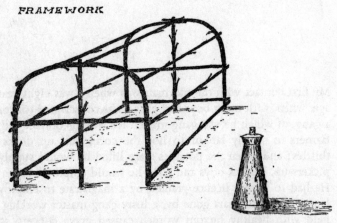

'NIGHT STORAGE HEATER'

FIG. I.

twelve feet high. Most of them were as thick as my wrist; there were six acres of these which when cut and peeled sold well as broom sticks, hoe handles, etc. Some of the slender long ones had a ready sale to be used as fishing rods. Job asked the farmer if he could have me to work with him, peeling the rods after they were cut. The first morning on arrival at the site of our future labours, he told me this was a job that would last all winter, and being in the most desolate part of bleak fens, and over a mile away from the nearest building, we would need somewhere to shelter in when the snow and rain came along. Having cut a number of thick

4

willow rods, he showed me how to strip the bark off with a paring knife, the bark coming away in long lengths about an inch in width.

Whilst doing this I watched the old man mark out an area eight feet long by six feet wide, then at each corner planted stout poles, also one in the centre of each end. These latter two were a couple of feet higher than the corner posts, for they supported the ridge pole. The tops of the corner posts were bent over and fastened to ridge; these forming a sloping roof. Sides and ends were braced with willow rods; also the roof (see Figure 1). All the frame work was fastened together by strands of twisted willow bark. The whole structure was then thatched with reeds. The door was a separate unit, its hinges being strips of dried

FIG. 2.

rabbit skin. When it was finished (see Figure 2) the old man said, 'It can blow, snow and rain; inside that lodge we shall be as snug as a bug on a baby.' He also remarked that a thousand years ago there were several lodges (a lodge was the ancient name for abode) like the one he had just built, within a stone's throw of Ely

Cathedral. That was in the days when over-fed monks lived in stone-built houses and the half-starved serfs lived and died in reed-thatched huts.

We soon had a fire some distance away, burning dead stumps and peat. Job found an old discarded milk churn, red with rust, with a tight-fitting lid. When work was finished for the day the churn was filled with red-hot embers from the fire; the lid was clamped on and we carried it into the hut. After fastening the door we started for home. Next morning on entering the hut just as dawn was breaking we found it warm and cosy. When it was too wet to work outside I would sit enthralled, listening to the old man's tales of social history and folklore, pondering over the fact that maybe Job was the last of many generations that handed down for over a thousand years plans and elevations of an abode, made on the spot with local materials, excepting the night heat storage unit. Job ended his life in the bare cold workhouse, nearly seventy years ago, but I have never forgotten the lesson he taught me on how to keep warm when a howling winter blizzard swept over the desolate fen.

RATTY'S TALE

Ratty earned his nickname after he had set up as a self-employed rat catcher. He was uncertain of his age, reckoning he was about ten years of age when he first joined a whaling ship at King's Lynn as a cabin boy and blubber copper stoker. This huge copper stood on an iron foundation on the ship's deck. Through stoking it with coal, combined with smoke, soot and blubber grease, the boy's face with sea water fixed the hue which was to last him the rest of his long life.

After a few years he decided life on a whaling ship held no future for himself, so, in his own words, he 'swallowed the anchor'. Still retaining his rolling gait as he wandered around the countryside, he made a fair living catching rats on farms and buildings at a contract price of two pence per tail. Sometimes he would have a blank day, which, as he used to state 'no tails; no money'. That did not worry Ratty, for when he was ferreting the banks of dykes or an isolated corn stack, he would place purse nets over all the rat holes excepting the one the ferret used to bolt the rats. As the rats were driven out they would dash into the purse nets and the draw-strings would close them. Ratty would examine his catch; if a buck he would knock it on the head with his club; but if it was a doe he would grab it by the neck, work its tail through one of the meshes of the net and bite its tail off with

7

his teeth. He would then let it run off, for his belief was, never kill the goose that lays the golden eggs. But that little trick ended when the farmers found their dogs were killing a lot of rats with no tails.

Ratty moved over into the fens and launched out as a buyer and seller of donkeys, and, travelling around, he just made a bare living, for at the time donkey transport was dying out. There was one thing Ratty did not like, for if he went into a pub for his evening pint, one of the regular customers would say to the land-lord, 'You want to watch that bloke; he is a dickey dealer.'

One day when walking along the river bank, he made up his mind to forsake his crafty calling, saying to himself, 'I will lift up mine eyes unto the hills, whence cometh my help.' He made his way to where the man in charge of the river bank lived, telling that worthy, 'That bank is smothered with mole hills.' 'I know it is,' replied the man, 'the snag is, the mole catcher we used to employ has gone underground, but he did not have to burrow like the moles; a hole was dug for him and since then the whole banks are riddled with mole hills.' So Ratty, in return for three-pence per head for all dead moles, took the job of killing them off – and he did not do badly for in addition to three-pence for the corpse, he skinned them, receiving from a skin merchant three shillings per dozen. This meant, for a year or two, lashings of beer for Ratty. Then the river bank, weakened by mole tunnels gave way and the whole fen was flooded. Ratty had just time to sling his ferret box on his back and, with his digging spade on his shoulder, made for higher ground.

Finally, he reached the edge of Breckland in Norfolk, where a farmer, on hearing his tale, allowed him to sleep in the hayloft. Next morning, on being told by the farmer that his farm was part of a large estate, he advised Ratty to go and see the agent, who was looking for someone to kill off the rabbits. The agent agreed to Ratty's terms – four pence per head for all rabbits delivered to the estate office. As the estate was swarming with rabbits, Ratty moved into lodgings at a pub in the village, where, in the evening, with a good day's work behind him, he was able to do a bit of homework as a beer shifter.

One day, on delivering his catch, the agent said, 'You know

8

that wood with a moat around it? It is called the Haunted Wood; probably it is, for there are some very old ruins there. Now, the boss says it is teeming with rabbits and he wants you to thin them out before the shooting season starts.' Ratty had to cross the moat by a wooden foot bridge. In the centre of the wood was a large area of brick and stone rubble, covered with ivy. He looked at it ruefully and thought, 'It's a risk putting ferret down there.' Then, looking closely at a heap of soil outside a newly made burrow, he saw what looked like a piece of dirty tin. On picking it up he found it was very heavy for its size. Rubbing it on his trousers, he found it was gold. On turning over the soil, with his spade, he found a lot more of the dirty metal objects and by the time dusk had set in he had unearthed a fair sized heap.

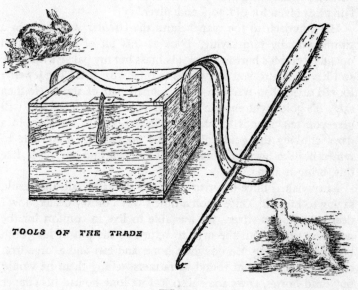

TOOLS OF THE TRADE

FIG. 3.

One by one he took his ferrets out of the box and turned them adrift down the burrows. As he did this, he said to himself, 'In a year's time there will be no more rabbits here because the wood will be full of polecats, for these ferrets are half-bred polecats.

Two bucks and two does; they will quickly revert back to wild state, and, by inbreeding, their litters will be polecats.'

Ratty then filled the ferret box with the bits and pieces of the metal he had found. When he slung the box on his back, he was aware it was as much as he could carry. Calling on the agent, he told him, 'That wood is haunted; not by ghosts, but by hundreds of black adders.' He went on to say that he had lost the tools of his trade his ferrets, so he was clearing out to a place where there were no black adders. Wandering around, he came to an empty tumble-down cottage. Finding out the owner, an agreed rent of a shilling a week enabled Ratty to become an householder. There was a river close by, where he was able to wash his finds. Amongst the gold were silver and pewter. There were no questions asked when he walked into a shop which had a notice in the window, 'A fair price given for old gold and silver.'

His approach to the man behind the counter was made in a simple way by him saying, 'Look at this bit of metal I found outside a rabbit's burrow. I say it is brass but my pal says it's gold, so I have come to you for you to tell me what it is.' The jeweller looked at it, then weighed it on a small pair of scales. He then said, 'It's gold right enough; do you want to sell it? If so I will give you ten pounds for it.' Ratty walked out of the shop in a daze, clinking the gold coins in his pocket, but quite able to remember the jeweller's final words, 'If you find any more like this, bring it along.'

Ratty visited three other towns, with the same tale and result, saying to himself, 'Once upon a time I was a dickey dealer, now I deal in gold and silver.' He was able to live in comfort for the next few years, until the urge to return to the job of his youth became too strong. He bought a horse and cart and a large iron copper. Then he went round to farmers, telling them he would buy dead horses, cows and sheep. Before long he had his copper going, boiling up dead animals. At frequent intervals he would skim off the rising fat, for which there was a demand as cart and waggon axle grease. I used to visit him now and again to listen to his yarns, and although Ratty was quite happy with his job and surroundings – I must admit – the stench of burning fat from an overflowing copper, the reek of coal smoke and the general aroma around the scene, distracted one's mind as Ratty related one of his tales.

Over sixty-five years have passed away since Ratty stoked up his copper for the last time. Now, as I sit gazing into the blazing fire on a cold winter night and a gust of wind forces the smoke down the chimney, I only want to get a small whiff of the acrid vapour to see pictures in the glowing embers, of Ratty relating one of his stories of local folklore, as told to him by his grandmother in the days before he went to sea.

BY
ROYAL COMMAND

Witches in north-west Norfolk played a real part in the lives of folks living there from the fourteenth century downwards. Folk tales handed down verbally from one generation to another proved again and again that an aged old woman living alone was sure to be a witch well versed in the arts of black magic and other tricks of the trade which enabled them as co-partners of the devil to play on the fears of the people.

One of the witch-ridden places was Castle Rising. Here, in 1614, the Earl of Northampton founded Trinity Hospital, where twelve poor widows or spinsters could live together, receiving a dole of six shillings a week. A governess was also provided to keep them out of mischief. Naturally the Earl thought by herding the old gals together, and feeding them well, they would forsake the devil and all his works. Besides coals and medical attendance they were provided with clothing; this, among other things, included a tall cone-shaped hat and a long black cape. Little did the Earl think by choosing that hat and cape for the women to wear, he was setting the pattern that was to become the traditional dress for witches all over the country. Neither did he take into consideration what would be the result when twelve garrulous old dames living in close contact started a merry-go-round by holding covens at the bewitching hour of midnight. Folk tales relate that, in due course, covens of witches were formed in not only Castle Rising but also in the nearby villages.

There were several wise women living around Sandringham when HRH the Prince of Wales bought it in 1863. These wise women he cleared out. He also pulled down the old cottages and replaced them with modern dwellings, to house the estate employees. One old woman was allowed to remain, in the nearby village of Flitcham. Even the newly appointed agent to the Prince of Wales dared not turn her out, for not only was she supposed to have the power of putting a curse on people, she was also reputed to have a vast knowledge of herbal cures when other remedies failed. She would wander miles in search of a certain herb she required. Lots of folks sought her aid when they needed a starter or stopper in time of distress.

As the years passed by, His Royal Highness as a hobby built up a stud of thoroughbred horses. Inside Sandringham House he collected a number of thoroughbred ladies. As a result of having to keep one eye on the brood mares in the stables, and the other eye on the females inside the house, demanding a share of royal favours, his health broke down; this in 1880. He was very ill for a considerable period. Princess Alexandra sent for her sister-in-law, the Grand Duchess Olga of Russia. When these two ladies met, the topic discussed was what could be done to get His Royal Highness out of the low state into which he had fallen, so that he could return to a full-time filling of his favourite pursuits. Both ladies feared that ordinary medical efforts had failed, and both agreed that another opinion should be sought; also that the only way to get the Prince back on his feet was to use the Danish belief in the supernatural, combined with the Russian inherited faith in sorcery and black magic. Discreet inquiries down the social scale revealed the fact that some of the kitchen staff had good cause to be grateful to an old woman, a supposed witch, living at Flitcham, for getting them out of a muddle due to wandering off the narrow way that single women were supposed to walk thereon.

In due course the old woman was commanded to appear before the Princess, who suggested perhaps the old woman knew of some remedies that would help the Prince to recover. The old woman replied: 'I can give you a bottle of wine which I have made myself. Give the Prince three glasses a day, and within three days – unless he is in the undertaker's hands – he will be sitting up in bed.' Four days afterwards a groom from the royal stables brought the old woman the news that the Prince of Wales was getting better; also, would she give him three more bottles of wine to take back. He also handed her a purse containing gold coins. The folk tale ends here but, over fifty years ago I was in Flitcham, and being in need of refreshment I called at the Bell Inn. During a short conversation with the landlord, I inquired about the wine woman. He informed me that the old woman had been dead for years, a long while before his time. However, if I wanted to know about her I should stand that old man dozing in front of the fire a couple of pints of beer and he would supply all I wanted to know. Having placed a frothy pint in the old man's hand, I asked: 'Do you remember that old wise woman that used to live here?' 'Yes, I do', he replied, 'I was only a young man when she was about. My mother and she were real old cronies. Few people called in a doctor when they were queer; they all went to the old gal, and I still remember what her brew of rue tea was like. It was nothing less than liquid gunpowder, and everybody said it was so powerful it would shift a traction engine. She had a lot of cures in her house, some in jars; others in bottles. She used to make a lot of home-brewed wine, which she never drank herself. Her drink was gin. She used to come to the back door of this pub, knock a couple of gins back and take some home in a bottle. One day, when she was a bit tiddley, she showed my mother a handful of gold coins. She boasted they were given to her by the Princess of Wales, in return for supplying bottles of her special mandrake root wine when the Prince of Wales was very ill. The old gal also supplied the gentry with this wine; it being a well-known fact it was just the stuff to supply a much wanted energy.' I left the old chap drinking his beer, and as I cycled homewards, I came to a steep hill, so I said to myself: 'To climb that hill one needed a bottle of mandrake wine.' Halfway up, there was a pub, where I tarried for a while, to drink to the memory of the wise woman of Flitcham, who was in full agreement with the advice St Paul gave; to take a drop of wine for the stomach's sake. Probably also that

old woman was aware of the story mentioned in the Bible, of
Jacob sending his womenfolk out into the fields to collect
mandrake roots so that when he grew old he would be well
supplied with male and female labour on his farm.

If we are to believe that Jacob knew the virtue of mandrake root
being a go-getter, one must admit that writers of late nineteenth-
century social history were at fault in not recording for posterity
the fact of the part played by the wise woman of Flitcham and her
bottles of home-made mandrake wine.

BEE LORE

'Telling the Bees' is an old custom or ritual perhaps little understood by many newcomers to bee-keeping today; understood but not believed by a lot of present-day but older bee-keepers; but nevertheless practised by very many bee-keepers of long ago and who have departed from this scene. That is, if the many writings on the subject are to be believed. Those writings indicate to us that whenever an important event – be it a birth or death – occurred in a bee-keeping family, the bees have to be informed of the fact; otherwise they fail to prosper and, even worse, they die or flit from the scene. In the case of a death, the bees are informed by someone of the family visiting the then often skeps of straw, in turn, and quietly voicing the information, even to reciting appropriate verses. Moreover, pieces of black cloth or crepe would be draped over each skep. This custom continued up to and into the days of the wooden hives.

One evening a number of years ago, I was on my way to give a talk on some aspect of bee-keeping. I was accompanied by a bee-keeping friend. He was also an undertaker, or, in present-day terms, a funeral director. The conversation ranged over various aspects of bee-keeping and during the course of the conversation, he volunteered the information that he regarded his prime job as being 'a service to mankind'. He went on to say that on one

occasion he had to conduct the funeral arrangements of an elderly
bee-keeper and when it was over he went back to the house and
asked the somewhat incapacitated elderly widow whether in the
circumstances she would like him to 'tell the bees'. He told her
that he did not altogether believe in the custom but did respect
the sentiments of those who did. Having obtained her grateful
assent, he passed on the information in as sincere a manner as
circumstances allowed because, as he said, he was able to put
himself in that lady's position, and to himself it formed part of
his dedicated service.

Of course the modern bee-keeper would say that were bees to
die after a bee-keeper's passing, it would be because there would
often be no one to hand to give them attention, and, telling or no
telling, they would die of starvation. This often did happen
because strange as it may seem, it is not often that more than one
member of a family takes to bee-keeping. Often, too, there is one
cause for this – the fear of being stung.

A casual remark by another bee-keeper friend to the effect that
he had a good mind to put a hive of bees near his meadow gate to
discourage people who persisted in leaving open his meadow gate
brought a desire to delve into the possibilities of bees having
been used in the past for aggressive purposes. Having heard that
hives or rather skeps of bees had at one time been used in a kind
of sling for hurling into a mass of human invaders and that a
picture or drawing of this was in existence in the library of Christ
Church, Oxford, I wrote to the librarian – the date was 25 May
1949 – and at the same time asked whether he knew of any other
instances of bees being used in warfare. I received a reply to the
effect that a drawing was preserved there. This was in a document,
and was by one Walterus de Millemet, of the year 1326. It was in
the form of a windmill and skeps were placed at the ends of arms
contraptions, which on being revolved would sling the skeps
outwards (centrifugal fashion), from which the bees would
escape with, it is presumed, dire results to the enemy. The
librarian informed me that he did not know of any other instances
of warfaring bees.

Researching again, I noted that it appeared that the first time
bees were used in warfare in this country was in the region of

908 BC. An army of Norwegians and Danes, with aggressive designs on Chester, came by way of Ireland to attack that place. Commencing by attempting to undermine the city walls, they fixed hurdles for protection against rocks hurled on them from above. Additional stout posts put in to augment the hurdles caused the defenders to pour down boiling mead and water. This, in turn, was counteracted by covering the hurdles with thick hides. Not to be outdone, those resourceful defenders gathered together all the hives of bees on which they could lay their hands. They then threw them 'overboard', with, to them, gratifying results, for we learn that: 'The desired effect was achieved, for, being badly stung, the enemy abandoned the siege in despair.'

Similarly, various like instances are recorded down history's ladder, not forgetting one which occurred during World War I. It appears that in East Africa, in November 1914, a force of soldiers under Brigadier-General Aitken, attacked a party of Germans. The latter, by way of retaliation, hid a number of occupied hives in scrubland, near the route which it was expected the Brigadier's force to travel. All went as planned as far as this scheme was concerned; the hives being pulled over at the right moment by attached wires which were operated from a distance. It is recorded too that although well and truly stung, the victims did not turn back.

It was a case of the tables being turned in the instance of a small party of Belgians being under attack after having confined themselves in a place where bees were kept in some quantity. Germans were the aggressors. After preparations, the Belgians 'withheld their fire' until the attackers were within range near enough for them to throw bodily the occupied hives towards the enemy. This time, so it is recorded, the well-stung enemy was repulsed. Perhaps that enemy's consoling, in more ways than one, ointment could be found in the lines:

> He who fights and runs away,
> Will live to fight another day.

Perhaps too, with due acknowledgment to William Harrod – Hempsall, perhaps the greatest researcher in bee-keeping this country has ever known, one more instance of bees being used

against humans – en masse – will prove of interest. I quote from
what he has also quoted from another work; it being concerned
about the scene of the bees' activities at Basil House, St Clether,
Cornwall, at that time the home of the Trevyllian Family:

'The building, which is in perfect repair, forms three sides of a square, with
double arched gateway for the main approach. Judgement for a large sum was
obtained in Supreme Courts, so the story goes, against the last of the Trevyllians,
the execution of which he defied. A posse (of men) was sent by the Sheriff to
levy on his goods and apprehend his person. He barred his doors within the
courtyard, but left the gates open. The officers rode in and demanded admittance
to the house. Trevyllian spoke to them from an upper window, and advised them
to be off or he would send his spearmen against them. They jeered at the threat.
Trevyllian caused the great gates to be closed and secured.

In a room on one side of the quadrangle was sheltered a large number of bee
hives, the openings in the loop-holed walls allowing the insects to go in and out.
Trevyllian gave orders for the hives to be upset and all other openings closed. The
bees in their fury swarmed out of the room through the openings and attacked the
Sheriff's men and their horses, who were stung to madness. At last Trevyllian
allowed the gates to be opened, when the whole posse fled.'

In passing, it should be mentioned, that closing entrances to which
bees had access would in itself make the bees angry because being
frustrated upon return to their normal means of access, they
would attack anything moving within the vicinity – in particular
horses, because the smell of the latter, particularly when perspir-
ing, incites them; likewise goats, humans, sundry scents, weather
conditions, sounds, temperature conditions; to sum up, something antagonistic to their accepted way of life, and one bearing in
mind that there is always a reason for bees stinging, because they
surely do not embark on this light-heartedly; when just one bee
stings it stings but once – loss of the sting and the life of that bee
ensues.

As a bee-keeper I have often been asked whether I get stung.
The answer must always be: 'At times – yes!' It is possible to
handle bees individually or en masse without getting a single
sting. On the other hand, particularly with regard to modern
methods and in large-scale bee-keeping, a time-table and a set

system has often to be worked, irrespective of some adverse conditions. That is where the skill and resourcefulness of the experienced 'keeper comes in. Invariably, protective clothing is worn, but over the years, nevertheless, a bee-keeper will get a good peppering with stings. The saving grace for the majority is that most bee-keepers become immune to any after effects through this long-term inoculation. At the same time there are some people who are allergic to stings.

I recall the instance of one person who received but one sting, on her leg, behind her knee. Within minutes a rash similar to nettle-stinging appeared. The doctor was telephoned. He advised getting straight to bed; a cup of hot tea; he would come straight-away. When he arrived perhaps a half-hour later, the rash had nearly subsided and all was well. But the lady had been warned. She was not one for continuing bee-keeping.

With further reference to nettle-stinging, for some reason best known to others with more skill in other fields than bee-keeping, it is a fact that a person well-stung over the years through bee-keeping hardly notices a sting when affected. Stings from nettles, on the other hand, last with itching for upwards of three days.

It is gratifying for a bee-keeper to know he is not allergic to bee stings. I remember being asked by the widow of an elderly bee-keeper to examine her or rather his bees. There were ten lots. It was getting towards the end of the season when bees were not at their best. They had been neglected for several years. I collected an average of ten stings from each lot during that Saturday afternoon, with no ill effect other than some slight itching.

On another occasion – on almost the last job I did in the role of disease inspector for the Ministry of Agriculture – I examined in the one day, unavoidably near the end of the season, no fewer than forty colonies of bees. As each of the ten combs of bees per hive had to be taken out and the cells examined, it can best be imagined how many stings were collected that day – many more than the previous example, I know. So, to finalize, 'Telling the bees' may be a relic of the past but they will it is expected continue to 'tell you', in their inimitable way, for many years to come.

CURING WITCHES

It was Saturday evening and the landlord was reading aloud extracts from the weekly paper.

'Listen to this', he said, '"Three hundred years ago a witch was boiled alive at King's Lynn."'

'They shouldn't have done that.'

The words came from an old man who up to then had sat silent, nearly asleep.

'That worn't the proper way to treat a witch. I know a better one.'

A full frothy pint was placed under his nose.

'Drink that up, Grandfather, and tell us.'

The landlord retired to the cellar to fetch two gallon cans. These he placed on the table and then proceeded to collect the price of two pints from each of the expectant listeners. There were going to be no cash-and-carry interruptions while old Dad was telling his story.

'What I am going to tell you about,' he began, 'happened just after the flood that drowned the fens in 1861. An old woman lived in a tumble-down shack down Sedge Fen drove. She was so old she remembered being at the Battle of Waterloo. How she got there was like this. She'd married a soldier and in those days a soldier's wife used to go along with him to cook his grub and look after his kit while he was fighting. Her husband worn't killed in that battle but he wor in another one, so she came down here to live, taking up the job of a firster-and-laster, unpacking infants when they came into the world and packing up the old ones when they went out.

'Then she got so old and dirty people wouldn't hev her. She used to go around the fen threatening people with her curses. If a farmer saw her looking at his pigs and one was a bit queer afterwards he didn't send for the vet – he sent for the butcher to turn it into pork before it got worse, being certain it had been bewitched.

'The old gal was well aware of what people said she was, for children, after getting safely past her, would shout "Witch! Witch! Get home, you dirty old witch!"

'She managed to exist and buy black shag for her short clay pipe on the few shillings she picked up by frightening people. One of her best paying tricks was this. People opening their door first thing of a morning would find on their doorstones a heap of loam shaped like a grave mound. It would be of sandy loam and as all the soil round about was black peat it could only have come from a distance.

'Then the old gal would come along and say it was put there by the devil to let them know it wouldn't be long before he came to fetch them. She often met him carrying a sack when she was out at nights, she would say. And, being wise in the arts of that old black one, she could, for a shilling, remove the curse the devil had put on the house. After getting the money, she would spit on the heap, then tell the people to let it lie there until the next new moon. They could then gather it up and put it on the garden for the worms to play with.

'Now, up in the village lived Billy Brown. He never did any work unless obliged to. But he managed to get along quite well for there wasn't a better poacher going.

'One night – it was getting near Christmas – Billy had been out and the bag he was carrying was a bit heavy. As he neared home, which was down Church Lane, he heard the clock strike twelve, then through the hedge he saw a light moving about in the churchyard. His eyesight was just as good among the tombstones as it was in the woods and he soon saw it was the old gal carrying a spade and a candle-lantern.

'Peering through the hedge he saw her set down her light and kneel beside a newly made grave. So he nips home, dumps his bag, gets hold of his old muzzle-loading gun, rams a charge of powder into it, then pours in a handful of saltpetre crystals that he used for curing rabbit-skins down the barrel, wadding it well home with paper. He worn't long getting back up the lane where he could see her shovelling soil of the grave into a sack. She had her back to him, and her behind it was bobbing up and down as she got on with her job. It was a lovely target in the flickering light of the lantern.

'"That will larn her", said Billy to himself as he pulled the trigger.

'On hearing the explosion and feeling the impact of the salt-petre she let out a hell of a shriek and leapt up into the air, kicking over her light as she came down. People living nearby, having been awakened by the shot and the shrieks, opened their bed-room windows, then dressed themselves and in a short period gathered on the road outside the churchyard gates listening to the unearthly din going on inside. One of the waiting group was the sexton, who on being told he got paid for looking after the churchyard and that it was up to him to go in and find out what was the matter replied:

'"That may be so but that's day work, not night-shift, and the only one who ought to go and see about things is the parson as he gets more money out of the churchyard than I do."

'So he said he would go and fetch him. He arrived at the rectory and threw a handful of gravel up to the rector's bedroom window. The rector put his head out and wanted to know what was the matter.

'"Matter!" said the sexton, "You come along and see. The church-yard is full of shrieking devils and the smell of brimstone and sulphur is enough to choke you."

'The rector came down and opened the door, then, seeing his sexton was shaking like a leaf, poured him out a drink of whisky and, not knowing what lay before him, had a double himself. Then, just in case his sexton was right, he put on his surplice,

23

grabbed a big stick and, with a lighted lamp in his hand, joined the waiting people, suggesting some of them should go with him and help to turn the shrieking devils out. He soon found they were all of the opinion that it was a job he could best manage alone, being well up in the knowledge of what bell, book and candle could do.

'Calling for his sexton was in vain, for that worthy, not knowing what demands might be made on his services, had returned to the rectory where the rector in his hurry had left the whisky bottle on the table. The sobbing of the frightened women and the trembling of the windy men convinced the rector that if he did not get a move on he would soon be in the same nervous condition as they were. So he opened the gate and, firmly grasping his stick with the lamp out in front, he strode down the path, keeping his courage up by shouting: "Get out, you swine!"

'Then by the light of his lamp he saw a woman in black holding on to a tombstone with one hand and rubbing her posterior with the other. She, on seeing something in white coming towards her, let out a terrific yell and ran down the path as hard as she could go, falling head-over-heels into the dyke at the bottom. The rector tore after her, stumbled over a grave, gave his nose a nasty smack on the stone kerb and lay still. His lamp, after rolling a few yards, exploded, sending a sheet of flame into the dark sky.

'Billy, thinking it was time he had a hand in things, had crept through the hedge, entered the unlocked church and, getting a bell rope in each hand, pulled away for all he was worth. The din the bells made was too much for the frightened jackdaws in the steeple. Out they flew and, attracted by the lanterns held by the people in the road, swished their wings a few feet above their heads as they circled in the darkness.

'Billy, creeping back through a gap in the hedge, was just in time to see the old gal crawling up the dyke to the lane. Getting behind her, he gave out a yell which sent her running off again until, on reaching the road, the prickly heat was so bad she sat down in the grit and tried to get ease from the terrible itch by sliding backwards and forwards.

'He then went up to the waiting people, wanting to know what sort of a game they were playing at that time of night and why

24

they were not in bed. He was quickly told what had fetched them out was a lot of devils having a party in the churchyard. The rector had gone into turn them out, they said. The doors of hell had opened and they had seen roaring flames gushing out. As the rector had not returned they reckoned by this time he was nothing else but cinders and that swishing noise above their heads was made by those devils who did not get back before the door was shut.

'"Well, well", said Billy. "That must have been one of those devils with a hurt wing that I nearly fell over down the road. I'll go and fetch it."

'So he went and picked up the kicking and spitting old crone, setting her down among them, saying:

'"I've caught this one. Hold it and I'll go and see if I can find another."

'It was not long before he returned holding up the sexton who was so drunk he couldn't stand. So he sat down and wanted the people to repeat after him the words of the burial service which he knew by heart.

'Billy, finding that all those standing around were firmly convinced the rector had gone to that place he had warned them about on Sundays, borrowed a lantern from one of them, telling them it was the black sheep of the flock that was going in search of the shepherd, for when he had last met the rector they had parted on unfriendly terms. It was just after Billy had returned home after serving three months' hard at Norwich Castle for poaching. The rector had told him he was a disgrace to his father and the village. Billy had assured him he knew he was a disgrace to his father in getting caught after all those lessons he had received from the old man on how to avoid it. As for the village, the parson might spend a month white-washing his parishioners but most of them would still be piebald.

'Finding the rector lying between two graves and smothered in blood from his bleeding nose, Billy sat him up and told him how surprised he was to find him fighting drunk and in the churchyard at that and wanted to know what had happened to the other chap, as he must have been in a terrible mess, too, with all that blood flying about. All the rector could do was to hold his aching head

25

and promise Billy that if only he would help him to get home he would do anything for him within reason. A bargain was quickly made that in return for help the rector would buy from Billy a brace of pheasants every week while the game season lasted.

'By the time they had reached the road there was nobody there. The old gal had told them that while she was kneeling gathering midnight dew from a new-made grave to cure her warts there was a big thunderclap and lightning had struck the path, spattering the place she used when sitting and making a real gravel rash of the whole seat. They were so wild on hearing this that they carried her to the horse pond and threw her in and as the sexton was now well away praying for those at sea they gave him the same treatment.

'Then they all went home. The sexton soon sobered up and went too, but the old gal was still sitting in the cooling water at noon next day when the parish beadle came along and pulled her out to take her to the workhouse.

'So you see', concluded the old man, taking a long drink, 'there's no need to boil a witch. Just pickle their hams like Billy did. That will cure them, especially if you do it with saltpetre.'

THE GHOST OF
BAWBURGH CHURCHYARD

'The Ghost of Bawburgh Churchyard' saw the light of day in 1909 and was the brain-child of one F. V. Cole of the little village of Barford, one of the cluster of villages a few miles west of Norwich. As far as can be ascertained, he lived a simple and homely life. Of use to the community around him, he did for at least part of his life travel in pony and trap, selling household commodities, groceries and packaged flour to the villagers.

Unquestionably, he had a literary turn of mind which, amongst other outlets, resulted in his efforts finding a haven in the columns of the local Press, often consisting of nature note records, the happenings around him and the like. Later in life he too had a bed-ridden spell but this did not put a full stop to his writing activities. (In actual fact he had been bed-ridden for twenty-eight years prior to his death – this when eighty-three years of age – in his Barford, Norfolk home. Altogether Fred V. Cole had written over one thousand articles for the local Press. The last one – a nature effort – appeared in mid-October, 1939.)

Strange though it may seem, of the few elderly people seen and plied with questions regarding activities of F. V. Cole, not one remembered him as a result of his writings. Instead, the mental picture they recalled of him was the one enacted many times, that

27

of the pony quietly plodding along on the often homeward journey from Norwich, where he obtained many of his wares, with reins hanging loosely and the 'driver' sitting hunched up, oblivious to the world and people about him, doing of all things, reading a book. Indeed he was of a literary turn of mind; indeed, too, he had confidence in that free way of travel which would be totally misplaced and out of question in these days of over-crowded roads and lanes. The poetic turn of mind bears fruit in 'The Ghost of Bawburgh Churchyard':

THE GHOST OF BAWBURGH CHURCHYARD
A true story

1 If now, as in the days of old,
  Each country side possessed a bard,
  Some poet would ere this have told
  Of our churchyard.

2 In verse that would have made the name,
  Of our loved home, old Bawburgh's vale,
  Rank high upon the roll of fame,
  A true ghost tale.

3 But as the tale is left to me
  In simple language to rehearse,
  If with the story you make free,
  Excuse the verse.

4 'Twas in the days ere Bruce's law
  Had placed a check on drinking men,
  Or Cross had barred the alehouse door
  At stroke of ten.

5 One night as clocks were striking twelve,
  That hour when ghosts, 'tis said resort
  To human haunts, and merry elve
  Holds woodland court.

28

6 Three merry wights, who had been filling
   Themselves with drink, and th' alehouse till
   Which of their pence, full many a shilling
   Had gone to fill.

7 While they each other's ears refreshed,
   In maudlin tones, with gossip's tales,
   Were standing at the tippler's rest,
   The white bridge rails.

8 Where one must leave his bosom crones
   And makes his way towards his cot
   Down New Road, past the heap of stones
   Which mark the spot.

9 Where once, upon the village green,
   A hermit dwelt, so gage and hoary,
   Past the hall gate, so oft the scene
   Of ghostly story.

10 To which a brood of sucklings white
    Which chanced some rev'ler to surprise,
    Of white bull calf, or great owls flight
    Has given rise.

11 Now, o'er the bridge the other two
    Proceed with slow and swagg'ring gate,
    Heedless, discussing something new,
    Though 'tis so late.

12 While trees, and rails, seem gliding round
    Until the Stocks' hill green they reach,
    Their noisy talk the only sound,
    Save owls' harsh screech.

13 Or water mill's incessant rumbling,
    Here they must part, one climbs the hill
    At its unusual steepness grumbling,
    Or standing still

14   To shout another farewell word,
        While the tramp of his comrade's feet
        Fainter, and fainter still, is heard
        Far up the street.

15   But 'tis the latter we must follow,
        No gossip now his steps retard.
        Towards his cottage in the hollow
        Through the churchyard

16   The churchyard gate is reached at last,
        He passes through, then hastes along,
        The chancel door he hurries past
        Humming a song.

17   Then home in sight, he has just gained
        The old church porch, when wild with fright,
        His weak drink shattered nerves are strained
        At that dread sight.

18   For there within the steeple's shade
        A dreadful being meets his eye,
        His song is hushed, he stands, afraid
        To pass it by.

19   His boast was that, his country's foes
        He'd faced on many a battle field,
        And not the sight of death's dread throes
        Could make him yield.

20   But now his tottering legs refuse
        There wonted duties to fulfill,
        So that he cannot even choose
        To stand quite still.

21   For every tale that he has heard,
        Of this lone spot, at this dread hour,
        Comes to his mind, with solemn, weird,
        And magic power.

22   That seems to thrill his very bones
As on the ground he trembling falls,
And there behind the nearest stones
He quickly crawls.

23   The drunkard, when he tries to steep
His poor brains in his favourite cup,
Will tell us that 'tis done to keep
His spirits up.

24   And others, who so temp'rate live,
That to suggest they drink is treason,
For their wee drops will often give,
The same good reason.

25   But here's our friend, who has been taking
Sufficient drink to make a hero,
Behind a gravestone hiding, quaking,
His pluck at zero.

26   How long he was constrained to hide,
The village gossips ne'er have told,
Though some have said he would have died
Of fright and cold.

27   Had not there sounded loud and clear,
Sometime before the break of day,
Resounding sweetly in his ear,
A donkey's bray.

28   The bolts and bars that many a time
Have grated on the prisoner's ear,
May sweeter sound than evening chime,
When freedom's near.

29   So without friend, this donkey's bray,
Which oft had hindered his repose,
Was music now, and strange to say,
His courage rose.

30 Then from the ground he quickly rises,
    Nor stays he longer at his post,
    While slowly he soliloquzies,
    'Is this the ghost

31 That I can now so plainly see?
    Is this what caused me such a funk, eh?
    Four legs! what ears! say can it be
    My master's donkey?'

F. V. Cole, Barford, Norfolk, 1909

MELTON GHOSTS
AND OTHERS

Villages linking with the picturesque village of Bawburgh (this latter being but three or so miles west from the City of Norwich) are the two Meltons — formerly known as Magna and Parva respectively; now commonly Great and Little. From time to time some of the elderly folk of one or the other of the two villages would intrigue any willing listener with snippets of tales of local ghosts which they in turn had heard from there own forebears. Unfortunately they could not recall full details; unfortunately too they have passed on, thus rendering any memory jogging impossible.

Fortunately someone had the forethought to put something in relation down in writing; this as early as a hundred years ago; in 1875; in a yearly periodical known as *The East Anglian Handbook*. How long before this date the tales applied can only be conjectured. However, there was formerly a curious legend told amongst those Melton folk, how earlier a bridal party, driving along what was known as the old Norwich Road, were accidentally upset into a very deep pit, so deep that it was reputed to be bottomless. The unfortunate people were never seen again, at least, not in the flesh. Nevertheless every midnight and every noon a carriage drawn by four horses, driven by a headless coachman and footman and containing four headless ladies in bridal dresses, rises, all dripping wet from the pool. This outfit careers silently around an adjoining field then just as quietly sinks again into the pit.

At the bottom of what was known as Coldblow Hill in Great Melton is a fine old beech tree. It is possibly nearer three than two hundred years old. It is still a well-known landmark and I understand the subject of a preservation order. It is said that the spot was once a meeting place for some of the harriers. Be that as it may. The fact is that until recently there was a useful wooden seat fixed beneath the copious spreading branches where many a passing traveller on foot along the Norwich to Watton Road took a short, well-earned rest. However, the mystery is why, many years ago, should a woman of ghostly appearance sit there precisely at midnight, with a small child in her arms, rocking herself to and fro, in apparent distress? Alas! no one is now alive to supply an answer. Could it be the result of a tragedy arising from activities of smugglers, reputed to have operated in the adjoining village of Marlingford, also those many years ago? Maybe someone, somewhere, has written something down to give a linkage.

Little Melton lane (the one now known as 'Rectory Lane' fits the story) is also reputed to be haunted by a tall man in black. He springs from the adjoining marl pit upon belated travellers. Perhaps this is a local equivalent for the Erl King (or Oak King) of Danish mythology, who dwelt in the innermost recesses of the forest and thence lured unsuspecting travellers to their destruction.

It seems a pity to destroy a person's belief in a ghost story by supplying a solution. Between the two wars the instance arises concerning a man who was travelling late one Sunday night from the place of the family he visited in Long Stratton along the Ipswich Road to Norwich; a journey of some ten miles. When he arrived at the bottom of Dunston Hill (check for yourself via a map) he saw a white object towering a bit above a five-barred field gate. This gentleman did not keep this experience to himself because a few days later a letter from him on the subject appeared

in a local paper. In it he emphasised that he had had no strong
drink before leaving for home – 'only a healthy cup of cocoa'.
Obviously he was mystified and concerned.

But a day or two later still, another letter on the subject
appeared in the same paper. In it was the explanation that the
'ghost' was in fact a white cow; that the horns which appeared to
have jutted from the ghostly head were real, as indeed were the
mooing sounds which had issued from the 'ghost' at the relevant
time the traveller had passed. Whether the traveller believed that
explanation is not known. What is known is that the facts were as
given by the compiler of the second letter; none other than the
present writer's own mother, who lived, as did he, but one
hundred yards from that gate and where they had waited many a
time for the local bus to come along, thus giving opportunities for
looking around and 'seeing what's what'.

She is in her mid-eighties now and she told me a tale of a
happening over sixty years earlier, not long after she was married.
A sister was spending a holiday with her and her husband. Not far
away lived a young man who was courting the sister and in
furtherance of this pursuit visited the family each evening. It so
happened that the nearest way was through the churchyard. One
night the husband thought he would play a prank on the ardent
swain, so he posted himself behind the graveyard wall. Upon
hearing approaching footsteps, he made a timely rise – with a
white sheet over his head. The young man turned and fled. The
'ghost' disrobed and quietly sauntered home.

Later, the young lady, getting worried at the non-appearance of
her young man, asked her brother-in-law to go to her lover's
home to find out what had happened. He did so and after
unsmilingly listening to the young man's story of his alarming
experience, together with the resolve not to go through the same
experience and way again under any circumstances, pleaded
successfully with this young man by offering to act as escort and
guard. He did this on subsequent occasions. What he did not ever
do was to enlighten his grateful escorted companion of the part he
played in the episode.

JOHNNY AND JENNY

Several years after his mother's death, Johnny lived alone in the two-roomed shack in the Methwold Fen, obtaining a fair living out of the rich deposit of turf his few acres of holding provided. Spring and summer he was busy digging and drying the black bricks of peat which in the winter found a ready sale in the surrounding villages.

His water supply was a dyke in which a dark brown liquid slowly made its way into the main drain. Using this peaty coloured water for laundering and ablutions had tanned both his linen and features a deep russet brown. To prevent his innards being tinted the same hue, he never drank tea, but quenched his thirst with a drink he bought in bulk from a brewery, conveying the barrel home in his turf cart.

Although he lived a solitary life in an isolated spot, he never shunned his fellow men, being always willing to share the warmth of his turf fire and the contents of his tapped cask with wayfarers passing that way.

Johnny was in his late sixties when a female came into his life. It happened in the following manner. One night at dusk a band of gipsies with a donkey cart came down the drove, put up a tent and camped a few yards from his dwelling. Johnny, after making sure his door and window were securely fastened, made up his fire, loaded his gun and, telling the old collie dog stretched out on the hearth rug to keep on the alert, retired to bed.

A few hours later the growling woke him up. As he lay listening to the rustling of the sedge covering on his turf stack he surmised the gipsies were making a midnight raid in order to obtain free firing. Silently he opened the window, but it was too dark to see what was going on. All he could hear was the carefully stacked turf tumbling down.

Aiming his gun in the direction of the noise, he pulled both triggers almost at once, making a terrific bang which echoed over the fen. He closed the window and sat on his bed listening to the commotion going on outside. It sounded as if someone was in pain.

It seemed hours before the groaning ceased and he heard the sedge grass rustling again, accompanied by a champing noise as if something was eating the thatch. After a time he heard the rattle of a water bucket outside the door, then a gurgling sound as if someone was taking a drink, followed by the sound of footsteps getting fainter and fainter.

When daylight came he went outside to have a look around. The gipsies had gone, so had some of the thatch. Some of it had been trampled into the mud upon which lay a new-born female, naked in the chill dawn air. Picking it up, he carried it into the house, placing it in front of the fire, where it lay whimpering and trying to suck his finger in search of nourishment. Having nothing in that line to offer, Johnny set off across the fen to a farm a mile away. The farmer and his wife who had been up all night on 'Home Guard' duties were surprised at his urgent request for a quart of milk. Knowing he was no tea drinker, they wanted to know what it was for. Johnny told them how the gipsies had given him a bit of a fright in the night, and said he thought if he went off the beer and switched over to milk it would steady his nerves up a bit. The farmer promised to help in the cure by putting him on his list of regular customers.

When Johnny arrived back home he put the milk into a saucepan to warm up over the fire, then went outside and cut a long length of hollow reed stem. One end he placed in the milk; the

37

other into the hungry mouth. Ere long the youngster was fast asleep.

This method of rearing the lusty female continued for several weeks. Then, finding his daily round getting irksome and seeing she was eating a bit of roughage, he tried the contents of the cask as an alternative drink. He found she took to the beer like a duck takes to water and soon learnt the knack of drinking from a mug.

He christened her Jenny and watched her grow into a handsome creature. She had such small feet that her shoes had to be specially fitted by a footware specialist. Her large expressive eyes reflected all the misery and hardship her ancestors had suffered down the ages.

When she was old enough Johnny took Jenny along his turf round. He found her useful when serving his customers, of whom the best paying ones were the inn-keepers. One of the tricks of the publican's trade was making sure a good glowing fire was always burning in the room where drinks were served. Johnny would tarry a while basking in the warmth his merchandise provided. Jenny, tiring of the long wait, would move along to the next tavern. Since it was not the custom in those days for females to enter pubs, she would stop outside, demanding refreshment with a brazen voice. Her wants were quickly supplied, for she had many admirers who were glad to pay to see her knock back a pint without pausing for breath.

All the children adored Jenny. Sunday school treats meant her being run off her feet as she did her best to entertain them. As the years passed by, her company was sought by a wide variety of people. Then any woman in a hurry to get birth would call for her assistance. She was also known to assist the undertaker with his transport problems. If a sailing yacht was becalmed, she would, with a rope round her shoulders, tow them for miles down the river. Local preachers with an appointment at a chapel miles away in the fens were glad of her company as they wended their way along the droves, rehearsing the sermon to her attentive ears. Sometimes two preachers would travel together and when the spirit moved them would burst into songs of praise. Jenny would turn the duet into a trio, ending up as soloist.

Sometimes the homeward bound journey would provide the

opportunity for her to add a comic touch by stopping at a wayside inn, then refusing to budge another step until her escorts procured her a generous sample of the brew.

Besides making life's journey easier for others, Jenny loved the good things nature provided. An open garden gate was to her a pressing invitation to enter. Sometimes she had to depart in a hurry, for some gardeners resented her intrusion on their privacy.

Probably owing to the gipsy strain in her blood, she hated policemen and when the young enforcer of the law gave her a playful smack, she showed her resentment by giving him a kick that put him on the sick list for over a fortnight. On his return to duty he warned Johnny that he would run him in if he did not have a stricter control over Jenny's behaviour.

This little comedy of village life reached the ears of those in authority and the arm of the law was transferred elsewhere at which the fenmen rejoiced. It was natural, therefore, that when Johnny took Jenny up to Southery Feast both should be offered a lot of free refreshment. Then as the naphtha flares were dying down, Jenny made her way through the milling crowd in the stall-lined roadway and Johnny swaying somewhat from side to side acknowledged the many shouted 'Good nights'.

Jenny, weaving from one side of the drove to the other, at last reached the bridge over the drain where supper and bed awaited. Next morning tracks shew where Jenny's vision had misled her, so that she had tried to cross by the bridge that was not there.

At the inquest on Johnny details were given of recovering the two bodies and a dicky cart from the deep water drain. As he had no relatives few people attended Johnny's burial but before Jenny was buried scores of people came to see her lying in state. It was the chance of a lifetime for very few people had ever before seen a dead donkey.

THE GAME-KEEPER AND
HIS DAUGHTER

She was tall, big-boned and of ruddy complexion – as was to be expected of a daughter of a game-keeper born and bred in the northern part of the country where the often harsh elements made the men, and women, the tough characters they were more often than not. White haired she was too but in spite of the threescore years and ten she was nearing she retained a quick wit and a sense of humour which belied the fact of the hard and sometimes harsh treatment she had received in the impressionable and early days of her life. Lack of educational opportunities – she had but six years of schooling – helped rather than hindered the moulding of her character when launched at an early age into the seas of after-school life.

Both her mother and elder brother passed away when she was quite young but not too young to remember them just. She retained all her life some of the incidents relating to her father and mother. Father, working in a game-keeper's role on one of the not-over-large country estates at the time, was fond of his beer and would at times go from public house to public house perhaps too often than was advisable. Perhaps there was no harm in that, but again too often the poachers would work all the harder when they knew where he was. Later, because his employer also knew, he paid the penalty by being dismissed. Not even his wife's pleas (unknown to him) with his employer could change the decision, even though the latter knew he would be parting company with a game-keeper who was a master of his job when it came down to 'brass tacks'. Thus started what was to be one of perhaps too many moves to fresh estates and new faces. Yet he was a more than average likeable man – in spite of at times of uncertain temper – handsome and what some would call a gay lad; resourceful too.

Came the sad day when his wife passed away, after but six years of marriage and leaving him with two small children of tender age. This taxed his resourcefulness to the hilt but he proved equal to it; even if some of his efforts proved at times somewhat unusual. On one occasion, noting that his daughter was not putting on the weight he thought she should, he gave her a dog worm powder which for a short time produced results that caused even him alarm. As time went on, and the task of 'keepering and bringing up two children became more exacting, he accepted his mother's offer to have the children for a time. In due course, because the lonely game-keeper's life became even more lonely, he searched around for a wife; found one; married her. Unfortunately he omitted to tell her he had two children.

One day he had a letter from his mother asking him for more money towards the keep of the children. He did not think it necessary to tell his wife; just stuck the letter in his pocket. A while later, his wife found that letter. She put it on his dinner plate when he came in for his meal. An explanation was of course sought and eventually given. The outcome was that the children were brought home to their, now, step-mother. Later still, the game-keeper's son died.

The daughter of the first wife was not liked by the second wife. When the first child of the second wife came along the now handy-in-household-chores daughter bore brunt of both work and lashing of the tongue. She also at times feared her father. On one occasion she received a belting from him for too thickly peeling the potatoes. Uncertain of his actions at times too the daughter related how when he found one of the doors locked he fired his gun into it at close range to successfully break down the lock. On another occasion the mother told the step-daughter to get a pail of rain water from an outside tub to heat for a bath. Out she went with the pail – it was night time – and as she passed the hen-house, she heard a scuffling; dropped her pail in fright; ran back into the house and told her step-mother. The latter, although small, was not deterred. She grabbed a stick and a light, went to the hen-house and on opening the door, found her husband picking some hens off the perch and putting them into a sack. He laughed at being found out; said he was after some ready cash and was told off severely for his pains. Next day, as if to belie what he had said about shortage of money, he put several pounds on the mantelpiece for his wife, as was customarily done after he had had a row with her.

On another occasion his daughter came into a shed when he was packing something into a hamper. Later, when he had gone, she went back, opened up the hamper and saw a layer of pheasants. Underneath was a layer of hares, with yet another layer of pheasants underneath that. While she was looking, her father came up quietly behind her and gave her a resounding smack across her ear. Half-crying, she asked her father why he was doing this. He told her he was packing them up on behalf of the estate. Later, this somewhat inquisitive daughter found out that they were going to an uncle, who kept a game shop. Later too, she found a hamper had been packed with mushrooms but thought she had better not ask any questions.

Another lucrative source of income came from tips of money from the invited guests of shoots. These were often as large as five pound notes, which proved two things – that he was a good game-keeper and that diverted loads of game in hampers were not missed. After one of these shooting days, one of the guests saw the little girl sitting outside apparently taking an interest in the things going on around her. Approaching her, he asked:

'And who are you?'

'I'm the game-keeper's daughter.'

Then, out of the blue, unexpectedly from that little girl, came:

'Do you swear?'

'No, my child, of course not.'

'Well! my father do – and he's a bugger at it too.'

Another way of making extra money was to take in dogs to train for later use as gun dogs. He would have two at a time, at a charge of five shillings each a week. For one of the exercises he would fix a belt round his waist, to which would be fastened, one on each side, the lead of each of the two dogs. Each lead had a quick release. He would then set out on a walk, with the dogs straining along a bit ahead of him. At times he would instruct them to 'Sit'. He would also carry a loaded gun. When any disturbed small bird – sparrow or blackbird – would rise, he would shoot at it, then quickly release one of the dogs, for them to retrieve the fallen bird and bring it to his feet. On one occasion he omitted to release the dog, with the result that both eager dogs started off in abrupt fashion. Caught unawares, the 'keeper was pulled over, to be dragged a few yards before gaining control, to the undisguised merriment of his watching daughter. Predicting trouble, she just as quickly stopped but her unpredictable father responded by taking up a loud 'Ha, ha, ha', where she left off.

No reason for smiles was there on the occasion when his wife, on opening a room door, found her husband examining a somewhat battered face close to a mirror, with the table lamp held somewhat precariously even closer to his face. Furious because he had just had a brush with some poachers, in which he had come off second best, he turned on his wife after she had slated him about the dangerous way he was holding that lamp. Holding it high over his head, he threatened to throw it from him and set fire to the house. At this juncture his daughter, hearing the raised voices, rushed in, grabbed the lamp and took it from the room to safety. Next morning some more pound notes found their way on to the mantelpiece.

Friction at home resulted in the daughter being sent out to service at an age when most children are still at school, and amongst the lessons learnt in the school of life were those of more hard work at home when, each time children were born to her step-mother, the 'keeper's daughter would be ordered home to do the chores until her step-mother could get about again.

Time marched on and the step-mother, with baby-hood demands replaced by perhaps less exacting growing children cares, said she would like to have an organ. Suiting action to her words, there arrived in due course, for forty pounds – saved from the money left from time to time on that mantelpiece – the welcome instrument. Nothing pleased her more than when, on a Sunday evening, with her children round her — her almost grown-up step-daughter, too — she played hymn tunes with concerted vocal accompaniment. No less pleasing were the times, though less frequent, when the 'keeper, stayed in and put a violin, hanging on the wall, to better use. This usually happened when he had little or no money to buy his beloved beer. His daughter remembered those times as being amongst the happiest interludes of her life while under the care of her step-mother.

All in all, the game-keeper's life was a healthy one; this in spite of the more often than not erratic hours having to be worked. Nevertheless, at times even he, big and strong man that he was, would feel a bit under the weather. The onset of a cold would be heralded by him peeling himself a number of onions, then boiling them to a cooked finish. Salt, pepper and vinegar would be stirred into that mass. He would then retire to bed, to eat his remedy while it was still hot, then with piles of clothes around him, stay in until he had 'sweated out' the cold. Less liked was the remedy given to the children in the spring of the year, a dosage of brimstone and treacle (sulphur and black treacle).

The years rolled on and came the time when the 'keepering activities had to cease. By this time the children had left the family homestead to in turn, build and feather their own nests. The 'keeper and his wife moved from the country into the town; into an old house, part of which — the upper storey — was used by home workers in the manufacture of lace and other products. To the occasional visitor, the subsequent noise of the working machines proved somewhat distracting, as indeed it did at first to the ageing couple. The 'keeper's daughter was a frequent visitor, having gained an even more close affinity with her father. As time went on, she noticed that he was getting frailer. He seemed to be pining for open countryside. Nevertheless, he would laugh and joke in his old accustomed way. He liked his pipe. Knowing this, his daughter, each time she called, passed over a half-crown for him to buy his favourite brand of tobacco. She remembered the first time she did this. At first he said he did not need any money for this. On her insistence he accepted it; with a sly smile about which she could not then fathom.

Eventually illness laid him low. He was getting near his end. Towards that end his daughter visited him. He recognized her but could not talk. After a while he succeeded in moving his arm around and pointed in turn to various parts of the room towards the floor, around which was heavy carpeting. His daughter failed to understand the meaning of his actions. Came the final moment but just before that he tried to raise himself and he framed a word with his mouth. This his daughter was able to understand. He had tried to call out her mother's and his first wife's name.

A short time after his passing, the game-keeper's daughter again visited the house. Her step-mother was in her late husband's bedroom – the one in which he passed away – and she was in the act of taking up the carpeting. While her step-daughter watched, she saw her take up one corner. Underneath was a small pile of paper money notes. Working her way round the edging, she retrieved other small batches. Tucking up her apron, she piled them into it and by the time she had completed she had gathered in what must have been a considerable sum of money; the exact amount the step-daughter was never informed. Nor did she benefit.

Thus the game-keeper's daughter learnt first of all of the reluctance of her father initially to refuse the small amounts she gave him for his tobacco and secondly, why he tried to draw her attention to the money he had hidden when she saw him in his dying moments.

The game-keeper's white-haired daughter rose from her seat on this sunny, late summer afternoon in the little country churchyard, where her mother lay buried, hundreds of miles from her father's last resting place. Yet once again she had made this annual pilgrimage. Slowly she walked along the edge of the churchyard to the gate, with her companion who had during the past half-hour listened to her relating some of her memories of the past. Suddenly, without warning, a gaily-coloured cock pheasant, in cackling protest, flew out from a nearby clump of withering grass. The game-keeper's daughter stopped in her tracks and intently watched this symbol of her earlier days get smaller and smaller as the distance between her and the bird increased, to finally plane with motionless outstretched wings low over a hedge into a harbouring field – a field which her father had many a time traversed in his early 'keepering days – and out of sight. Then, oblivious to the sacred surroundings and her watching companion, she murmured, with a faraway look in her moistening eyes:

'Aye! maybe he was a rummun at times but he was a good father; I hear his "Ha, ha, ha" now.'

POACHERS, CONVICTS, MANTRAPS

One often hears of Merrie England during the seventeenth and eighteenth centuries. For a very few of the upper classes it was a merry time. Heading the top of the list of large estate owners were former brewers, who amassed large fortunes contributed by the lower classes in the effort to drown their miseries in a potion made by boiling malt and hops, with yeast added to put a bit of guts into the watery fluid. These brewers bought up many of the large estates in East Anglia. The Enclosures Acts passed by Parliament during the reign of George III, 1760–1820, enabled them to fence in large areas, wherein the lordly pheasant was 'Cock of the Walk', closely guarded by numerous game-keepers, who ranked next to the squire and parson in social status. These game-keepers never went to church on Sundays. If they had done so, during divine service, their well-stocked game preserves would have become a self-service market for several poachers.

Game-keepers in those days were given the right to search anyone within the confines of the estate. This is where Toby Brown comes in. He was a casual worker, doing any job a farmer required. A lot of hemp was grown in those days, when hanging for theft was the law. Toby used to take a few sheaves of hemp from a farmer instead of wages. He would spin the hemp into twine, and besides making cordage and ropes, he would knit the twine into nets, for which he found a ready market amongst the local wild-fowlers.

One moonlight night he was taking one of the products to a man a few miles from his home. He was walking along the turnpike, which had a large wood on either side; quite unaware that new laws had been passed in 1816. One of the new Acts gave the penalty of seven years transportation for a man if caught with nets in his possession at night. Toby was within a half a mile from the inn where he was to meet a man to sell one of his nets, when he was grabbed by two game-keepers, who, finding the net on his person, gave him several blows with their cudgels, knocking him half senseless. After tying his hands behind his back, they marched him to the Hall. When they told the squire they had found nets in his possession, that he had put up a fight against being searched, that the blood on his face was the result of blows delivered in self-defence by the 'keepers, the squire ordered them to take Toby to Thetford gaol.

Eventually Toby was sent to Norwich Assizes, where the judge ordered him to be transported overseas for a period of ten years for committing the crime of assaulting the game-keepers and having nets in his possession. Toby pleaded he was no poacher; also he never had a chance to lay his hands on those two lying bullies. The judge told him to shut up or he would get another five years. He was taken to Woolwich where he spent three months in a prison hulk, before he was put aboard a convict ship bound for Australia. During the next five years he was in a prison camp, and in company with other convicts was hired out to a contractor who was building docks and making roads. Most of the time his work consisted of felling trees and sawing them into boards. He was fed on the barest of rations; getting no wages; spurred on by the overseer's lash.

Life was made more tolerable when he was moved up country to work on a large farm. Here he came into contact with a wandering tribe of aborigines, These natives often visited the farm, begging rye whiskey from the farmer. Toby had a ration of homegrown tobacco and, as he did not smoke, he gave it to the tribal leader. This gift was returned four-fold, for Toby was taught how to make a boomerang; also the trick of throwing it.

He learnt how to use a blow pipe so he could kill a bird with its dart. He was tutored how to walk bare-footed in the forest without a sound of rustling leaf or snapping twig. But the best lesson of all was how to freeze and conceal himself in thick undergrowth.

Toby hoped to make good use of all he had learnt when he was given his freedom, and thus after seven years of his sentence had been served he was given a ticket of leave, being allowed to go where he wished but not permitted to leave the colony. He went native for twelve months during which time he was taught how to find the gold nuggets concealed in the sand banks of a fast running stream. Soon he had a small fortune stowed away in his waist-belt. Then came the day, when, on reporting as a ticket-of-leave convict, he was told; 'You are now free, and if you care to return to England a free passage will be given.'

Toby returned home; bought a house with a few acres of land; married, and in due course became the father of a son. He named his house Botany Bay, just to remind himself of that convict camp at a place so named in Australia. Not being a lazy man, he was soon self-employed, killing off the game on the estate where he had been unjustly accused of poaching. Both game-keepers who had caused him so much misery went in fear of Toby when they heard he had returned.

Some time elapsed before Toby took his revenge. First one 'keeper, then the other, were laid out by violent blows on the backs of their skulls. They never knew what had hit them; but Toby did, for he was very pleased to test his skill with a boomerang. Both game-keepers went up to the Hall and complained to the squire, also showing him a large bump on the back of their heads. The squire replied: 'Get back to your job; as you stated, there was no one about; you must have been drinking and started knocking each other about.'

A while later the squire was out on horse-back when he received a blow on the back of his neck, causing him to fall off his horse. Found by a passer-by, he was carried home on a sheep hurdle. The doctor came in answer to an urgent message, that the squire was dead. The doctor said, 'He is not dead; the very thing

has happened which I have been expecting; he has had a stroke.'
Accordingly, the squire was put to bed, being kept there throughout the whole shooting season.

Toby kept the local game-dealer well supplied with birds. None
of them was shot-riddled; just a tiny hole where the blow-pipe
dart had entered. One night Toby was in the woods, looking up
in the trees for roosting birds. As he walked along he trod on a
concealed mantrap. Its steel jaws bit into his shin bone and he lay
there for two days before someone heard his cries for help. He was
taken to the small hospital at Thetford, where they took off his
smashed leg just above the knee. On coming home he made himself a peg leg of willow wood. The first time out he made his
way up to the Hall. This was in 1835. An artful lawyer had told
Toby that mantraps were made illegal in 1830, after when heavy
penalties were attached to their use. The squire paid up rather than
face a court charge, so, with what that gentleman gave him, and
the money he had saved, Toby settled down to a quiet life with one
leg and a dot-and-carry willow one.

When the son was old enough Toby started training him in the
ancient trade of getting a living without hard work. Before long
the lad became as expert as his father in the art of rustling game.
Toby had bestowed the name of Esau on his son, who was born
covered with hair – his wool, as his father called it. It provided
warmth when out in the woods on cold nights when, as often
happened, he had to lay up when 'keepers were about. He was
eighteen years old when out bird-watching one night and when a
'keeper's dog, having scented him, gave the alarm by barking
loudly. Esau decided to make a dash for freedom, being well
aware that if arrested he would be given a stiff prison sentence.
Leaping from the undergrowth he ran full tilt into a 'keeper who
aimed a blow at Esau's head with the butt of his gun. Dodging the
blow, Esau kneed the 'keeper at a spot where it would hurt the
most. As the 'keeper rolled on the ground calling for help, Esau
gave him a kick in the ribs for luck, then ran. Getting back home,
he told his father all about it. Toby thought for a while, then
went to the box where his money was stored. He put a handful of
gold coins into a leather purse, and said to his son: 'Take this and
clear out at once, unless you want fifty strokes of the cat-o'-nine-

tails with many years in prison afterwards.' Next morning the squire and four game-keepers made an early call at Botany Bay. Toby told them he had not seen his son since the night before. By mid-day the hunt was up; the quarry was miles away. He, in fact, was in London by nightfall, where he spent a few weeks in idleness. Eventually he enlisted in the army, and by doing as he was told, in two years had gained promotion; was sent to India, where it was very warm, with plenty of loot as he moved about the country. His stay there was all too short, for he was moved back nearer home, to Ireland, being stationed in Dublin. He liked the Irish, having been reared on home-distilled rye whiskey and finding the fluid the Irish distilled from potatoes being just as good.

Queen Victoria, to the Turks' delight, decided to have a bash at the Russians. This meant Soldiers of the Queen were herded like cattle into a ship, fed on salt junk and hard biscuits, then, after a long voyage landed in a bleak country and told to fight like hell for Queen and country. Esau did his share of fighting, robbing the dead and having two good meals a day of boiled dead-horse stew, until, one day, he was bowled over by a nearly spent cannon ball. He was taken to the field hospital; given a large dose of rum followed with opium pills, which sent him to sleep. When he woke up he found he was half a leg short. During his stay in hospital he saw no Florence Nightingales, only plenty of women the French had sent over to comfort wounded soldiers. As soon as he was able to travel he was sent home to Chelsea Hospital, and after a spell there, was discharged with a pension of a shilling a day and a couple of crutches. On returning home and to his father he found the squire was dead, so, bygones were bygones.

Esau's father gave him a piece of land on which to build a house. When it was finished he named it Sebastopol – where half of his leg was left. After a time his father died, bequeathing Esau money, land, and a wooden leg. When he started wearing the latter he gained another name – 'Pegleg'.

He was getting an old man when I first met him, and for a period he was my tutor of early eighteenth century social history and its folklore. If you want to know where he lived, just glance at a map of his district. There, tucked away in a triangle where Norfolk, Suffolk and Cambridgeshire meet, you will see these place names: Botany Bay and Sebastopol, and a short distance away is another place, Tasmania, where another ex-convict used to live. However, that man's life is another story.

ST ROCH AND RATS
AND OTHER THINGS

No one will now ever know whether the ghost of St Roch did indeed sidle up to the diarist Pepys during the height of the 1666 horrific fire of London and say: 'Samuel, ye fire warms my heart too', before vanishing into thin air again. Maybe Pepys was puzzled but he need not have been, for was not St Roch the Patron Saint of Plague? But Sam need not have been puzzled because some do say it was this very fire which put paid to the great plague which preceded it. St Roch didn't know everything about plagues as it turned out but he'd had a bit of experience. It is reckoned he was born in a place called Montpellier in France about – no one seems to get it nearer than that – 1295. It seems again that he had wealthy parents but when they died he decided that he did not want any truck with the horn of plenty, and, just like that other saint – Walstan of Bawburgh, near Norwich – gave it away to the poor people.

He travelled when past his two-score-years-and-ten to Italy at a time when a plague was raging and like the good man he had earlier shown himself to be he plunged into the midst of this peril, tending the sick and effecting what were then thought to be miraculous cures, both by physical contact and prayer. It is said that the physical contact was done by making the sign of the cross on the afflicted person's brow. Indeed when at Rome after being favourably received by the Pope, he made that sign on the brow of one of the cardinals with such effect that the impression could not be removed.

Alas! after doing this work for a long time, he himself became infected with that dreaded disease. He was in Piacenza at the time and although he had effected ministering care there, it brought forth no gratitude. On the contrary, he was given broad hints to find solace elsewhere.

Out of the town he struggled, eventually to wend his way to an isolated hut in a nearby forest. Alone, ill and starving, he had not the power to better his condition. Then, as if in answer to a prayer, an inquisitive dog sniffed its way to the hut. The subsequent actions of that dog saved Roch's life. Leaving the sick person, it went back to its master's house. Each day it removed portions of food from the rich man's table. Each day it took them to a lonely hut in the woods.

Eventually, its master followed it and, being a compassionate man, took the sick man to his own home and tended him until he eventually recovered. In due course he left that abode; wandered around again but with not much success in establishing a means of livelihood. Unfortunately because he was unable directly or willingly to extablish his identity, he was thrown into prison as a spy. Not for long was he there, because, from neglect or the after effects of that serious illness which had proved fatal to many others, he himself succumbed. He had earlier prayed to God asking for the favour of allowing all plague-stricken persons to be healed.

When the body of Roch was being prepared for burial, it was discovered, whether from identity papers on his person is not known for certain, that this tramp-looking person was indeed a member of a well-known family. Investigations into Roch's miraculous cures hitherto resulted in the acknowledgment that it was a saint's body which was now being disposed of. There were eventual quarrels as to where his remains should finally rest. Taken to his birthplace Montpellier, his body was later stolen and taken to Venice, where, it is said, a church was built to accommodate it. Just as people in widely separated places claim to own part of the crown of thorns of Christ; just as more than one person claimed simultaneously to own the mummified head of Cromwell; so do people claim in different parts to have the saintly remains of Roch. Moreover, it has been claimed that even parts of the body have found themselves dispersed throughout Christendom.

More down to earth down the years have been the investigations to find the causes of plague; plague which reached horrific heights of incidence from way back to the Black Death period in this country to shocking outcomes in places as far apart as Hong Kong and India. For a long time rats in some way were believed to be closely associated but it was not until 1894 during the Hong Kong plague during which it is said some 95 per cent of the population died that it was discovered that a bacillus – appropriately named *Bacillus pestis* – was the culprit. While infected rats could and did spread the disease, it was the fleas which infested the live rat on which attention was concentrated. Infected fleas readily passed on the bacillus to humans and other rats and animals by their characteristic biting. Be it the widespread bubonic or other types, the result was invariably fatal until knowledge of preventative measures built up over the years. One characteristic of a flea-infested rat was that when it died the lodgers flitted to other rats until the cycle was again repeated.

'Get rid of the rat' has been the cry over the centuries; 'Get rid of the rat' is still the cry. A prolific breeder – a rat will start breeding three months after birth – it can produce several litters a year, of seven to eight young on average in each litter. Apart from incidences of plague, a rat will foul and waste much more than it eats and some twenty-five rats will eat enough in one day to feed adequately one man. 'Get rid of the rat' then.

Poisoning, drowning in their holes, shooting, ferreting, gassing, snaring, killing with cats, killing with dogs, trapping – all have been tried, with varying degrees of success. Former rat catchers, known now as rodent and pest officers, still do their daily rounds in factory, house and on farm. Still the rats multiply sufficiently, if nothing else, to provide these folk with a full-time livelihood. In his small way the house- and small-holder still does his bit; as he did in the past. Poisoning was often effective – until some of the rats became partially immune as far as the required fatal effects were concerned. Invariably he fell back on his more reliable stand-by – the gin trap; always providing not one part of his bare hand touched it when setting, this being sufficient to warn off the keen-smelling rat.

I remember someone telling me some twenty years ago a story which revealed he wasn't exactly in love with the rat. Having recently moved house, he was able to gather quite a useful amount of apples for storing. Not having any suitable place prepared, he piled them in a large heap in an out-house. A few days later he had a look at them, only to find that the majority of those accessible had either been bitten into or fouled with their, the rats' droppings. Going outside he noticed that a pail of windfalls, left near a shed in the orchard, had been entered by a rat or rats, which had again bitten and fouled those apples. Trying to outwit those pests, he tied a rope to the handle then suspended it some two feet off the ground. To his surprise when he visited it the next morning he found that again rats had been at the apples. The reason, unforeseen, was in the pile of bee-hive parts stacked but a short distance away. Apparently Mr Rat had climbed these then jumped the intervening distance into the pail.

The cottager had his remedy. He set a gin trap on a few of the apples at the bottom of the pail, then suspended it as hitherto. Next morning he found a dead rat in the trap. On each of three successive occasions the ruse worked. Yet again did he try; this time he was grieved to find a blackbird had been trapped and because he did not gain much consolation from an instance of a blackbird, caught by a gardener in a wire-netting cage over some blackcurrant bushes, having no fewer than one-hundred-and-forty-three currants in its crop, he didn't set that gin trap again. Nor did anyone else who had hitherto used this kind of trap, because not long after that episode the use of the gin trap – last surviving replica of the larger even earlier abolished mantrap – was made illegal by law; this as from 31 July 1958.

ST WINNALD'S FAIR

First comes David; then comes Chad; then old Winnald as if he is mad.

Sixty years ago, some two months before these saints were due, loud curses could be heard coming from the farm stables where Hank was the team-man. The cause of all this blinding and swearing was due to the fact that Hank had just received orders: Captain and Punch, the two best horses in his charge, were to be conditioned up, so that on St Winnald's Day they would replenish the farmer's bank account which of late had persisted in a downward movement.

The two picked out for disposal had been in Hank's care since they were foaled; trained with kindness, whether in shafts or traces. They knew the meaning of every whispered 'Coupee' or 'Whooch', never having rein on bit except to comply with the law when on road work. Now, after eight years, they were to take a holiday and for a month or two would be housed in a warm straw yard, fed on best hay, soaked wheat, with a handful of linseed to make their coats shine. Hank spent most of his spare time with them, whispering to them as he polished their coats. On the eve of St Winnald he blacked and polished their hooves, rubbing the iron shoes with emery paper until they shone like burnished silver.

57

Before dawn next day he gave them a hot bran mash for break-fast, plaited their manes and tails with straw and gaudy ribbons. Putting new halters on their heads, he was soon on the road to Downham Market, where the annual horse fair, held under the patronage of St Winnald also attracted all the knaves and rogues who were past masters in the art of horse doping.

Gipsies with droves of Welsh or Exmoor ponies; Irish donkey dealers haggling with sturdy Norfolk folk over a dicky transaction; cheap jacks selling a twelve-bladed 'shut'-knife or a watch and chain for half-a-crown; quack doctors doing a thriving business on cure-alls at three pence a box; roundabout organs trying to drown the calls of the barkers – every one noisy except the pick-pockets, silently working through the crowds; horses and horsey men everywhere. Such was the scene when the auctioneer mounted his stand to declare the fair open. There was one, and only one, condition of sale – cash on the fall of the hammer, except to known clients.

Small ponies were sold first; most of these being knocked down to an undersized man buying for under-ground transport. The donkeys sold would spend the summer trotting up and down on the sands of the seaside. Hacks and vanners were mostly sold to provide tram, bus or cab motive power in the large towns. When all these were disposed of by the man in a grey bowler hat, 'gippoes', diddy-coys and the rest of the horse dopers now left the ring side, being replaced by prosperous men in breeches and leggings – no tricksters these hard-headed buyers for railway, brewery, contractor and miller. They had come from all parts of the country, because Winnald Fair was the best place to secure the heavy shire horse for draught work; all after the best that money could buy and each one knowing what he wanted and how much to pay for it. No haggling here. As fast as a horse was brought in, a price was named; the hammer fell and the next one was trotted in.

Captain and Punch were brought in together – two splendid black shires, perfectly matched and each one weighing over a ton. Proudly they tossed their heads as Hank led them round the ring and it was not the sun shining in his eyes that caused droplets of moisture to trickle down his weatherbeaten features. The auction-eer raised his hammer – 'No need to extol the virtues here,' he said, 'judge for yourselves, gentlemen; ever seen a better pair?' A contractor broke the hush by making a bid, to be followed by: 'Gentlemen, I am selling two horses, not ponies.' Came the 'Thank you' as the railwayman raised a finger. Then the brewer raised two, until, ding dong, the final bid ensured the two shires would haul barrels not trucks and leaving the ring to a farewell speech from the auctioneer of being the best pair of horses ever fetching the record price at Winnald Fair.

Hank, on returning home, informed all and sundry his two late workmates had gone to a good home; gave a week's notice; left his job and the neighbourhood.

A year or so later I saw him again. He was seated on a brewer's dray. Although he held a pair of reins, they were slack on the horses' backs and as I walked beside him through the crowded Norwich street, it was the same whispered 'Coupee' and 'Wooch' directing them as it had been done down in the fen farm. As I looked at the round happy face of the driver, the sleek coats of his team and the barrels behind him, I saw a picture of happy content and a perfect understanding between man and animals. I followed him to the place where those barrels were consigned. After he had placed on the nose bags, we entered the inn where in a short time I was told that after the horses were sold, the buyer, seeing how attached Hank was to them, offered him a job '– And here I am', said he. 'I get a lot more money than I did on the farm; all the beer I want – free. Captain and Punch don't have to work half so hard and like me, are well fed. What more does man or horse want?' 'Nothing,' I interposed, 'when they have such a patron saint as St Winnald.'

UNKINDLY LIGHT
LEAD THOU ME ON

Very few people living today can vouch for the following story, but it is true, and those who have seen Will of the Wisps or Jack O' Lanterns glittering over marsh and fen can vouch for the fact that in Heaven and Earth there are a lot of things which pass human understanding. Before modern drainage took over, a hot summer followed by a warm autumn created conditions whereby ditches dried up and large cracks appeared in a large area of fenland and marsh. These factors paved the way for a large display of those flickering lights which age-old folklore believed lured many folks to a tragic end. Those lights were due to marsh gas escaping out of the deep cracks in the soil. The gas exploded with a loud plop and as it reached contact with the air it burst into flame. I can remember many miles – square miles – of fenland all lit up on an autumn night, which struck terror into the heart of a young lad when told if one followed those dancing lights they would eventually end in drowning in river or dyke.

That was the reason many long years afterwards I was very interested in a tale an old man told me at Thurlton in East Norfolk. He was, as far as I could gather, the last in a line of ancestors that had lived in Thurlton for ages. Here is the gist of his story.

Up to the coming of the railway from Yarmouth to Norwich, the river Yare was the medium for conveying goods between those two places. Most of the traffic was conveyed by wherry, a type of boat which was confined to the Norfolk Broads and rivers. Most of the wherries were crewed by the owners. Loading and unloading were carried out by outside labour. As the wherries only sailed in daylight, there was a demand for mooring at night and one favourite spot for this was at Thurlton Staithe. In those days there was a hard road across the marsh from the turnpike to the river. Near the junction of turnpike and marsh track stood the White Horse Inn, which had been there since 1665. There, in the evenings, the wherry men sought respite from a lonely life spent on the river. Besides drink, the inn also provided meals, and as there was no restraint on opening and closing, those wherry men spent a large part of the night in drinking and yarning. Some would go back to sleep in the tiny cabin on their wherry; others would prefer to sleep in a comfortable feather bed provided at the inn. There was one man whose home was in Thurlton who would leave the company to sleep with his wife. A lot of money was being made in those days, when the country was at war with France. Freight rates on a river run were trebled between Norwich and Yarmouth. The latter place was sending a lot of stuff overseas, and as the result of so much money floating down the river, the wherry men decided to form a club, with its meeting place at the White Horse Inn. It was here they met once a fortnight for dinner and a booze-up afterwards. It was during one of those eat and swill evenings that the Thurlton man stated he would have to leave the gathering, because he had promised his wife he would bring back some things she wanted from Norwich. This meant he would have to go to his wherry to collect them. A latecomer to the party said: 'Anyone trying to cross those marshes tonight must be daft. I have been a long time finding my way here. It is pitch dark and the Jack O'Lanterns are popping off in hundreds. As one light dies down, another one flares up. I lost my way twice. The first time I was back again at the river's edge; the second time I was stopped by a dried-up dyke, along which there seemed an untold number of Jack O'Lanterns floating about. I was mighty glad when I saw the lights shining from this pub's windows.' The Thurlton man, after drinking a double hot rum, said: 'Goodnight to you all: I will be seeing you in the morning. I'm not worried about

FORMER *WHITE HORSE INN*
THURLTON NORFOLK

FIG. 4.

those Will of the Wisps; I know the old marsh too well for them to lead me astray.'

At daybreak the men were back on their wherries, and, as they prepared to sail away, remarks were passed as the Thurlton man had not turned up. They reckoned his old woman was laying on his shirt, thus stopping him from getting up. A few days later wherry men were telling each other that a floating corpse had been seen going up with the tide nearly to Norwich and coming back again on the ebb tide. Once it had made the trip to Yarmouth, when, on its return, it was seen up the river Bure. Wherry men were riddled with the superstition that bad luck would follow if they hauled a drowned corpse aboard a wherry, or even touched it with a pole. Eventually a high tide left it stranded high and dry between Reedham and Breydon, where it was found by a man gathering drift wood. The drowned man was buried in Thurlton churchyard; the tomb stone on his grave still stands there, on which is carved in stone a Norfolk Wherry.

The old man ended his story by relating that on certain nights, when whirling sea mists from Breydon Water enshroud the marshes of Thurlton, a shadow figure can be seen wandering over the marsh, finally disappearing into the river. It is the ghost of the wherry man being led on by the Will of the Wisps or Jack O' Lanterns. Finally, the old man said: 'When I was a lad I used to attend the evening service at Thorpe church which stands on the edge of the marshes. One evening the parson kept repeating, "I will be a light unto your feet." That was the text he was preaching about. After he had done talking, we all stood up and sang:

> Lead kindly light amid the encircling gloom,
>> Lead thou me on.
> The night is dark and I am far from home,
>> Lead thou me on.

When we left the church there were hundreds of flickering lights all over the marshes; the escaping gas was putting up a very fine show. Later on, the river banks were raised; the marshes drained, which put out all the dancing lights, for they were never seen again. Now, with all this electric lighting everywhere, there is no need now to sing Lead Kindly Light.'

MISTAKEN IDENTITY

In 1971 an old man – he was in his early eighties – gave me a folder of sundry scraps of paper and music of old-time songs. Amongst these was a large sheet of paper headed 'L.N.E.R. Enginemen's Daily Record' with a reference including the year 1938. It appeared to be quite a comprehensive document for filling and one can well imagine this could have proved quite a burdensome record to complete after a day's work. This particular one was left blank. On the back, however, there was a different story – literally.

Closely written in pencil and not too clear to decipher in parts, was the following, with no apparent connection with the railway, mark you.

An English lady of title was suffering from a nervous breakdown. Having been recommended to stay in a German village in the mountains, she, knowing no German, went to secure the assistance of the local school-master, who had a smattering of English. Having secured what she wanted, she returned home but then remembered she had omitted to inquire if there was a W.C. attached to the house which the kindly school-master had been instrumental in obtaining. She therefore wrote for particulars as to the W.C. but as the host to be had never heard of the abbreviation he did not of course understand it. He in turn consulted the local school-master who came to the conclusion that the lady was a devout

64

church-goer and wished to know where the *Wesleyan Church* was situated. He wrote the following letter:

Your Ladyship,

The *W.C.* is situated about seven miles from your Ladyship's lodgings in the centre of a pine forest amidst lovely surroundings and is open on Tuesdays, Thursdays and Fridays. This is rather unfortunate if you are in the habit of going regularly but you will be pleased to know that a number of people take their lunch there and make a day of it.

As there is a number of visitors during the summer I would advise you to go early.

The accommodation of the *W.C.* is excellent and there are eighty seats. The bell will ring before the *W.C.* opens. I strongly advise you to pay a visit on Thursday as there is an organ accompaniment. The acoustics of the *W.C.* are excellent and the most delicate sounds are audible. I should be delighted to reserve the best seat for your Ladyship and have the honour to sit with you.

P.S. Hymn sheets are provided and must be returned after use.

My wife and I have not been for six months and it pains us a great deal because it is a long way off.

Yours ——

ON AND OFF THE GOLD STANDARD

On entering the city one is confronted with the sign 'Norwich is a fine city'. Maybe it is, according to modern ideas, but just hark back to the days of King Charles I. What was it like then? Simply nothing less than streets packed with churches, taverns and slum dwellings. Of course there were gentry who herded together in one special area but, taken as a whole, the place was priest ridden, pest ridden, with semi-starvation being the lot of most of its inhabitants. Amongst the privileged section were the goldsmiths, who were money lenders, pawnbrokers, and bankers. These did a thriving trade.

News reached the city that Cromwell was besieging King's Lynn, and, having raised an army of hairy, hard-fighting fenmen, was preparing to march on to Norwich. On hearing this the priests in charge of the churches became panicky. Rushing to the goldsmiths to convert all the golden altar vessels into hard cash, they even pulled the gold threads out of the vestments to cash in to coin. Having so many sacred articles on their hands, and being aware that if Cromwell or his soldiers cast their eyes on that lot, the goldsmiths realized it would be 'Off the Gold Standard' as far as they were concerned. They decided to put both sacred and secular gold into the melting pot. Ingots of gold could be easily hidden, or transferred elsewhere. Then, when an influx of estate owners and priests came into the city, the goldsmiths decided it was time they cleared out.

Leaving one member of their guild in charge of future transactions, the others proceeded to Carrow Abbey, each one carrying his share of the gold. They surprised the priests there by telling them that owing to a war being on, all gold dealings were suspended. This was a sad blow to those priests, who were hoping that by selling some of their golden altar vessels, if things became worse, they would have a nice little sum for travel allowance if they wished to leave the country. They were glad when they were offered a nice bit of cash for one of their sailing boats.

The goldsmiths were soon sailing down the Yare on their way to Lowestoft. Leaving the Yare for the Waveney, they stopped for the night at Herringfleet. Next morning they learnt that they would not be able to proceed much further because Cromwell's troops had placed a boom across the river at Oulton. This meant they would have to travel by road if they wished to obtain safety with the Royalist troops at Lowestoft. The four of them were soon plodding along the road through Herringfleet woods; each one having his leather bag slung on his back, which left his hands free to use his sword, to defend his gold.

As the goldsmiths were nearing the small hamlet of Lound, they met a party of Cromwell's soldiers. During the ensuing fight one of the goldsmiths left the other three to get on with it, running down the road until he came to the village pond, into which he threw his leather bag. Still running, he made for the church, to seek refuge. A pike thrust from a pursuing soldier prevented this. A priest coming out of the church found him dying by the roadside. With his last dying gasps the goldsmith told the priest there was a bag of gold in the nearby pond. The priest did not attach much value to the whispered words at the time. It was only of significance when one of the village men came and told him that while he was hiding in the bracken he had seen three men slaughtered by the soldiers. The villager went on to state he had heard the officer-in-charge say that each man was carrying enough gold to enable all the arrears of pay due to the soldiers to be paid, besides leaving a good sum in the kitty to celebrate the capture of Lowestoft.

VILLAGE POND ~
LOUND SUFFOLK

FIG. 5.

Eventually peace was declared. Then, a short time afterwards, the local folks were frightened to see a ghostly figure clothed in white standing gazing into the pond at midnight whenever there was a full moon. In those days there was a tavern on the opposite side of the road. The tavern keeper had had a poor time during the civil war because he had been unable to obtain the malt to brew his ale. Now his customers, having worked from dawn to dusk, were afraid to visit his tavern, fearing they would meet the ghost, either coming or going, in the dark. To make matters worse, the tavern keeper's ale went sour, due to the long period between brewing and consuming. Now, he had a few hogs which roamed around, picking up scraps of food whenever they could find them. Rather than waste the sour ale, he filled up the hogs' feeding trough with his unsaleable ale. The swine made the most of this free booze-up, putting terror into the hearts of the people as they ran around squealing and fighting.

Having got rid of his worthless stock, the tavern keeper decided to have another brew-up, hoping trade would pick up as the evenings grew longer. This entailed sitting up all night to keep his brewing copper on the boil. Round about midnight he realized, that owing to evaporation the copper needed topping up with more water. His water supply was the village pond. Picking up a bucket and on opening the door, he found that owing to the moon being at its full, everywhere was as light as day. Moreover, he could see the village ghost doing something on the edge of the pond. Being full of fumes from a boiling copper of malt, he had that extra little bit of courage for tackling anything. He needed that water, so he walked up to the ghost and said, 'Nice night, isn't it, to do a bit of fishing?'; this because the ghost was holding a long-handled rake in his hand. He was quickly aware the ghost was none other than the village priest clad in his surplice. He told the tavern keeper he wore that at night so that the local people did not interfere with his fishing, because he needed the carp for his Friday's dinner. As the inn keeper filled his bucket he noticed the full moon was reflected in the water.

When the next full moon was due the inn-keeper sent word round the village that on a certain date at the sign of 'The Village Maid', besides good ale, there would be a free show at midnight

69

of the local priest trying to rake the moon out of the pond. At the appointed time the tavern was packed. The rush lights were put out; everyone crowded round the windows to see the ghost come along to do his moon raking. As they watched, they all said, in effect, the priest had gone off his rocker. All went to church the next Sunday, but the priest carried out his duties as usual in a normal manner.

After a time the priest went abroad. On his return, he brought back two Dutch gold-beaters and they spent several months gilding the interior of the church with pure gold leaf. So ends the folk tale of how golden vessels from the temples of Norwich, after being purged by fire and water, were once again placed to the 'Glory of God' in St John the Baptist Church at Lound, in Suffolk.

After hearing the story of the Moon Raker in The Village Maid, I walked up to the church. Its door being locked, I had to be content with a view of the altar as seen through the lepers' squint hole in the wall, but I did see enough to convince myself that here was one place which was surely still on the Gold Standard.

FIDDLER AND OTHERS

James Boast was his name. Fiddler was his nickname – why I do not know. He lived at Bawburgh and finished his days there. (He died in his eighty-second year.) He knew hard times. I paid him a visit on 10 September 1948 and he said he would be eighty years old in the coming month. Not only did he know hard times; he experienced ill-health too. He told me he had not been to bed for over forty years because of chest trouble. Not that one would have known it when once he got under way with instances of hard times, hard work and long hours. Nor was he alone in experiencing these in the days when the poor were very poor and the rich – well! they jogged along as they had done from time immemorial. Perhaps, he said, the best instance of one man who knew what long hours of work were was that of a person named Blyth, who he said was the father of one of his contemporaries – Eke Blyth. This man worked for years, from four o'clock in the morning until nine o'clock at night – for what pay he did not say – for seven days a week.

Mr Boast proved he had a good memory, by recalling many incidents of bygone days. He remembered seeing wheat dibbling in progress at the nearby village of Easton and described the method whereby the operator walked backwards, using a pair of dibblers (just like Old Job). Asked why the wheat was not broadcast,

71

he said that that method was useless because of difficulty in covering; also trouble with birds. He recalled how in his very young days he, together with his brothers and sisters, would go gleaning at Bowthorpe, where, incidentally, he said he was born. He went on to say that it was no use gleaning at Bawburgh because the corn was more efficiently raked. They would gather together the ears of corn with what straw remained and when as many as could be held in the hand were collected, they would bind or tie them together with straw. Then where possible they would cut through the straw bundle below the bond – 'sorta tida it up a bit' – then put the bundles of ears into a sack. As the nearest mill was at Little Melton (a windmill worked by a Mr D. W. Child) they would somehow have to get the corn there, to be ground into flour. More often than not, the gleaners took advantage of the offer of a horse and cart owner to take the stuff there, on condition he had the straw. Of course the people did not necessarily receive flour from the same corn they took in. If for instance they took in one hundredweight of ears and straw, they would receive an amount of flour which would of course be quite a bit less.

That this method of supplementing their meagre food supplies was necessary can be realized by the instance Mr Boast gave of one village labourer who worked for a Mr Hart. (This is the Mr Hart of Hart's Lane, Bawburgh, and a member of the Hartt family, if not the same man, who instituted the charity well-known at least to the older Bawburgh residents.) During a particularly bad spell when he tried in vain to get work once again from that gentleman, Mr Hart said he had none but if his former employee would care to take some swedes from the 'turnip' house, together with some nearby wood for cooking them, he would be welcome to do so. Mr Boast went on to say that the offer was of course gratefully accepted because 'not a morsel of bread itself had passed his or his family's lips for thirteen weeks, for such were the "good old days".' Mr Boast went on to say that when Mr Child bought Bawburgh Mill he, Mr Boast, understood that the mill at Little Melton was partly dismantled. When asked why, he promptly said: 'He would have had no opposition then, don't you see?'

There was some recompense, however, for Mr Boast recalled

how his own mother used to buy two stones of malt at a time, then make some ten to twelve gallons of beer. It would be brewed in a half water tub affair. Not everyone would have one, for, to quote his words: '– and if you were respectable, so to speak, I should lend you mine when I had finished with it.' Beer was considered a necessity in those days when the mowers set to work with their scythes to cut down a field of corn. Starting at five in the morning; whether mowing or otherwise, the workers would work until dusk at night.

Mr Boast well remembered seeing the sight of thirty-three mowers cutting a fifty acres field. First one would start. Then another would commence after the first one had covered a few yards. The next one would do likewise. When the first one had finished his length across the field, he would shoulder his scythe and return to the starting point, now of course further into the field. He, the first one, was the most experienced; known as the lord, he would set the pace and woe betide anyone who 'riled' him, for should anyone shout 'More rope', he would quicken his pace, to the discomfort of the slower ones. They had to keep up because the scythes of the followers could be dangerous. They certainly had to be sharp. One particular lord, when he heard that cry of 'More rope', would, when a next general stop was made for a swig of beer, go to a tin in his 'frail' basket, and swallow part of the contents. This was brown sugar. Such vigour did this impart to him that he would set to work and mow half-way across the field before stopping to whet (sharpen) his scythe. For obvious reasons, the others had to follow suit.

One thing to which the villagers would look forward during the summer was the strawberry feed. One of his contemporaries lived in the next village of Little Melton, one Horace Frederick Rooke (in whose former house this writer lives and named after him) who did market gardening. He grew a large crop of strawberries. When the main crop was over, the gardener would say, according to Mr Boast: 'You can all go in and have a feed for three pence.' And we did.

DARKEST EAST ANGLIA

It was during the second year of this present century, that I learnt of the bitter period of the hungry forties of the past century. It was due to the tradition that 'It's the poor that helps the poor', that sent me on an errand carrying a jug of hot tea to an old man who was sitting on a heap of large stones, breaking them into small pieces to fill up the pot holes on the parish road. Born in 1820, he worked hard for seventy-five years, having started work at the age of seven. Now living in semi-retirement, he was existing on three-and-sixpence parish relief plus half a stone of flour or bread, weekly. In exchange for this, he had to put in two days mending the road.

Whilst he was sipping his warm tea, he related what life was like in his youth, when most of his meals consisted of boiled turnips or cabbage soup. 'Gut fillers, they were,' he said, 'with no body behind them.' Black bread, when it could be obtained, gave energy, because the flour with which it was made contained ground wheat, barley and horse beans. In those days he lived in Suffolk, where the people were known as Silly Suffolks. They were too! When the harvest came along, and gangs of Irish labour arrived, instead of electing a lord of the harvest, as they had done for ages, they found the day of sickle and flail were over; their place being taken by reaping machines and threshing tackles. It

74

was the Irishmen who started to protest that these machines were taking bread out of men's mouths. Deeds followed words in an outbreak of smashing the machines. Gangs roamed the country-side during the nights, and farmers discovered in the morning that what was a valuable asset one day was, by the next, worthless scrap. Harvest operations came to an abrupt halt; came the period when the night sky was all aglow with burning fields of ripe corn. Dragoons were sent from Norwich to knock a bit of sense into Silly Suffolks' heads. Probably they did, but, being billeted in farm houses, it was only natural that the farmers' daughters and the serving maids, and even young farmers' wives, received a fair amount of military favours, in return for extra rations supplied by the soldiers. The Irishmen, the cause of it all, quickly left the scene, leaving the local farm workers with no money to buy food; nor employment to obtain some. Some young men, preferring dumplings to turnips, moved into Norfolk. Others enlisted in the army, having learnt by direct observation that women were aware that a red coat had more 'come hither' than a ploughman's smock.

'The winter that followed was one of the bitterest in memory', the old man said. Having moved into Norfolk, he was lucky to get a grave-digger's job. The churchwardens employing him paid half-a-crown a hole. It was easy work owing to the churchyard having been buried over a few times. The soil never had time to settle; loose soil was quickly thrown out. 'I was never allowed to go deeper than four feet, and the parson was always coming along to make sure, as he said, I did not disturb those that had gone on before. I shall always remember the last one I buried. She was an old woman living alone, who, hearing a loud clattering on the road, opened the door, and what she saw compelled her to run to a neighbour's, screaming out that the devil was coming down the road, breathing fire and smoke. She then dropped down dead; dying of sheer fright. The cause of it all was a traction engine; the first one ever seen in the district, which went into a farmyard to drive a machine to thresh the stack of wheat. The men, who always found work in the winter threshing corn with a flail, said that the engine was nothing less than the handiwork of the devil, to starve them out. Now, in those perilous times, no well-to-do farmer lived at his farm; he went into the towns, leaving a foreman in charge. It so happened that on the night after the threshing machine's arrival, the whole place, farm house, buildings and corn stacks went up in flames. The traction engine was blown to smithereens by the powder – gunpowder – placed in the fire-box. There was hell to pay when the horse soldiers arrived. I was dragged out of bed, kicked and clouted; then with several others was driven like sheep to Thetford. Next day we were dragged before a magistrate, then sent to Norwich Castle to await the next assizes. When the judges came along, all of us were herded into the dock, like pigs in a butcher's sty. The parson from my village came along, and told the judge that I was an honest, hard worker, and went to church, but the judge said that he didn't want to know about the Sundays. "I'm here to decide what he was like on weekdays, and in my opinion, like all the others from his village, he is a danger to law and order. The least sentence I can give them is three years' hard labour to be served here in Norwich Castle prison."' The old man remarked, as he related this: 'Thank God I was a single young man, with no screaming wife to add to my misery as I was hustled out of the dock and into the cells. Here I had time to think. Why did I move out of Silly Suffolk into the cruel Norfolk, where it seemed to me that just a few folks held reign, who believed God is on my side, and, bugger the lower classes.

'For two years I did my share of tread-milling. I was then given the job of latrine emptier. That was a stinking task, carrying wooden buckets and emptying them into a hole in the castle ditch, which hole I had to dig. One day a head warder came along sniffing. He then said: "You stink." I got his goat out when I replied that it did not take a wise man to smell his own dung. For that reply I was put on bread and water for fourteen days. By the time my punishment ended, those wooden buckets seemed as heavy as a couple o' hundredweight of lead.

'But bad times, like good ones, have an ending, and the day came when the Castle doors clanged behind me and I was free. I shall always remember that journey across Norfolk, to what to me was home. I picked up a tidy bit of cash by following the trade I had learnt in prison; emptying cess pits of privies, and when I arrived at Thetford I had enough cash to buy a new rig-out of clothes. I went to a quiet spot beside the river, Little Ouse; had a good bath; then turned my back on Norfolk dumplings and Suffolk turnips. I tramped to Yorkshire, worked there for several years and saving a bit of money married but did not have any children. Then, yearning for the flat country of Fenland, I came here, earning a fair living by thatching and general farm work. My wife then died and I was alone. When old age came along and I was no longer able to do a hard day's work, I went on parish relief after I had expended all my hard-earned savings.

'Well! my lad, that's an old man's tale. Now I must break a few more stones to earn my pay. I am leaving my hammer under a heap of large stones; you can easily find it when the steam roller comes here next week, so if you want to do a bit of machine smashing you can do.' After expressing his thanks for hot tea, he added: 'God is up above, so all is well with the world.' My answer to that was: 'How do you make that out, existing as you do, on near starvation poor law parish relief?'

WALKING, WORKHOUSES, WORMS

He was what our elders called a tramp but we boys called him a mile-stone inspector. Workhouse masters entered him in their books as a casual pauper. His name was Thurston, with relations living in Cambridge. He received a good education – for his parents were well off – but could not settle down. In his own words, his complaint was itching feet, and to cure this he had a regular beat, from Cambridge to Lynn; then on to Norwich; ending up again at Cambridge via Newmarket. In the summer he would vary his route, going to Ipswich, then down the Stour Valley to his native place. He would say that this gave him the right to the title of East Anglian Roadster. Probably this was so, but I knew he was a champion story-teller, for on a warm summer evening he would sit on the grass roadside verge and in a cultured voice would inform us lads in more ways than one.

'Cambridge', he said, 'was a very select place; full of snobs who would walk miles just to get a sniff of a professor's sweat. Cromer', he went on, 'was worse, but I never saw much of the people there, because as soon as I entered the town a policeman would step up alongside and keep with me until I left the town behind. Norwich was a fine place. It had two Strangers' Halls; one in the centre of the city, the other being the casual ward at the workhouse. I did not know what the first named one was like, but was well aware

78

what a Hell of a place the second one happened to be. I once spent a holiday at Great Yarmouth and was there for two months. The cause of such a lengthy stay was a runaway horse in a hurry to get home, and I, being in its way, was knocked down; the result being that both legs were broken. Being only a tramp, I was taken to the workhouse infirmary, and put into bed in a large ward, where I had twenty old men for company; all old fishermen, waiting for the pilot to come to steer them into the haven of eternal rest. From my bed I had a view – not a sea view – of a large churchyard, on which my eyes rested. I learnt a lot watching the grave-diggers. In the mornings they would dig holes. Planting took place in the afternoons, and they worked like blazes to fill in the holes so that they could knock off for early tea.

'The two months' diet of two slices of bread smeared with some kind of grease and a mug of tea for breakfast, a basin of skilly for dinner and two more slices of bread for tea, was not a fattening one, but that did not cause me undue worry. You see! I was used to walking all day with nothing other than water to stay me. Then, one morning, my clothes were brought to me, reeking of carbolic; having just been washed and still wet. An old man came and helped me to dress. Both legs being in splints I was of course unable to walk. I was carried on a stretcher downstairs into the Master's office, where I was told that Yarmouth ratepayers were tired of keeping me, so I was being sent home to Cambridge, where I was born. Then I was carried out and placed lengthways on the parish bier, which was used to move the dead ones to the churchyard. Two old men trundled me down to the railway station, where I was given a ticket and then wheeled along until I came to the waiting train. I was then laid on a stretcher and placed in the guard's van. On arrival at Cambridge two old men were waiting with a four-wheeled hand cart. On this they pushed me a very long way until at last I arrived at the workhouse. Here I found I was out of the frying pan into the fire.

'I was put in a lime-washed-walls ward, crowded out with dotty old men. There were women, dressed as nurses, who were supposed to look after us. Looking at their pock-marked faces made me wonder whether, at the time they lost their virginity, they were also deprived of all human feelings. I was not long in their care. When the doctor saw my legs still in splints he had me moved to hospital, where young doctors, having put me to sleep, set my bones in a proper manner. I was soon able to hobble about on crutches.

'A relation, hearing of my whereabouts, fetched me to his home. He owned a large tea-rooms in the town. One evening he asked whether my father ever told me how we came into the tea-rooms trade. I told him that all my father told me was that selling cups of tea and coffee had been the means of getting the Thurston family a good living for near on two hundred years. He said this was quite true and then went on to tell me about the Thurston who began it all in the year 1700. At that period there were a lot of coffee houses in Cambridge. The one where a young man named Thurston worked as a waiter was known as the Turk's Head. Here the Dons used to meet, in a large room upstairs. Undergraduates had the ground floor. All those meeting there were keen fishermen, so most of the talk was about large fish caught and larger ones which got away. One morning when Thurston the waiter was taking a walk beside the river Cam, he came to a gipsy boy fishing. Stopping to watch him, he was surprised to see that the line was hardly in the water before he was pulling out a fish; these being large ones, too. Such a feat staggered Thurston, for he was fond of fishing when he had the time, so he asked the gipsy what kind of bait he was using. The boy told him to look at some nearby small clay balls and went on to explain that they were the ground bait; also broke one open to show that, mixed with the clay were tiny red worms and maggots. Next came the showing a tin with worms and maggots; the actual bait he put on the hook. Thurston asked the gipsy whether he would bring along two dozen clay balls also a tin of worms of the like used. If he would bring them to the kitchen door of the Turk's Head early on the following Saturday morning, he would get five shillings. The lad agreed to do this.

'On the Friday evening the coffee house did a thriving trade, for heavy wagers were being laid on the favourites who had entered for a grand fishing match down the river Cam at Upware on the Saturday. Thurston's job was downstairs, serving the under-graduates who were busy making wagers. He approached one and asked what were the odds he was giving against Professor Jones winning the silver cup. The undergraduate made a derisive remark then went on to tell Thurston that he wouldn't mind offering twenty to one that the professor would not catch enough fish to weigh in. Thurston asked him to put this in writing. This was duly done. Thurston then offered him a ten guineas stake. After accepting the money the undergraduate had second thoughts – thought there could be something fishy about the business – so he went amongst his pals and placed bets at twenty to one on Professor Jones to win the cup.

'Early on Saturday morning as promised the gipsy boy came along with the bait. Thurston paid him; also told him to bring another lot the next Saturday. He then hurried round to the professor's house, and told that gentleman how he, Thurston, had watched the gipsy boy catch a lot of fish, explaining also how he bought some of the bait the boy was using. Further, if the professor used the ground bait, and baited the hook with the worms, he would certainly win the silver cup.

'Thurston stole a few hours from his work; borrowed a horse and rode down the river to Upware, where, in a tavern known by the sign Five Miles from Nowhere – No Hurry, bets were being laid fifty to one against Professor Jones winning the match. One of the men said it was impossible for a half-blind old man, who could only just see his float, to win anything. Meanwhile, Thurston waited by the scales until the weigh-in. After the gun had been fired to end the match, the fishermen came along. The professor, who had drawn a place one-and-a-half-miles away, was one of the last to come in. As he approached nearer it was seen he had a large leather sack over his shoulder. When he dumped the contents of the sack on the scales, it weighed four-and-a-quarter-stones. He not only won the silver cup; he got other prizes for most fish; heaviest fish; also a special prize for the largest fish. Thurston received two hundred guineas as a result of his wager. He also received a nice bit of cash from the professor for the bait; also, he was asked to provide more bait for a match at Coe Fen in a fortnight's time. The waiter arranged with the gipsy boy to bring the bait along. The boy arrived at the coffee house on Friday evening, explaining that his father was moving further away; this being the reason he had turned up earlier. Now it so happened that Thurston was very busy, so he told the boy to take the bait to the professor's house. Professor Jones was pleased to see the lad, and, after paying him, asked from where did he obtain such a lure which no fish could resist. The boy agreed to tell if the professor would promise not to "let on to me". Upon receiving the promise the boy went on to state that his father was a travelling tinker. The family lived in a tent and when they moved on, the tent was packed on to a cart drawn by a pony. It so happened that, one day in the winter, they were passing a gibbet, on which was a man, gone quite rotten. A lot of birds were pecking away at the earth underneath. The boy went on to tell the professor that he asked his father why the birds were pecking. The answer was that the birds were after worms. His father went on to say that if he wanted to catch fish, he was to get some of that soil because in that soil would be found thousands of little red worms. By throwing a handful or two in the river, any fish within smelling distance would rush for a feed and line up for the chance of swallowing the worms that would follow on the hook. The professor found it difficult to believe that the gipsy lad dug the worms from beneath a gibbet, but the boy went on to state that he got lovely fat maggots from the Caxton Gibbet also lots of little red worms because there were always two highway robbers hanging there. Of course there was another gibbet half-way to Newmarket, but only one swung there at a time. He also went to the gibbet at Waterbeach in the summer; the soil was always damp because it stood beside the river. He further explained that he had to get up early; if he did not get to the gibbets by sunrise the birds would have beaten him to it and collared the lot of the maggots which had dropped during the night.

'The professor's reaction to this was to tell the boy to take the bait back to the Turk's Head, because he had finished with fishing. Thurston did not in the least mind for he found other dons who paid well for the fish lure.

'Thurston made a lot of money and was able to set up as a coffee house keeper on his own account, and since his day there has always been a Thurston's tea-rooms in Cambridge. If you don't believe me, go to Cambridge, and there, in St Andrew's Street, you

FIG. 6.

will see Thurston's tea-rooms, packed with college lads during term time. Just go in and say that Ike Thurston said I was to have a free tea, BUT DON'T MENTION WORMS.'

Then the tramp stood up and said: 'That's the end of my story. Now I must get along to Ely workhouse, where I shall be given a hunk of bread and cheese; also a bath — and a bed. Goodbye.'

A FEN MYSTERY

No one knew who he was. He first appeared in the fens, when, with other Irishmen, he came to help with the harvest. When the others left, he stayed on, living in a derelict cottage, shunned by the men, avoided by the women. It was rumoured he had the power to cast an evil eye and was also gifted with second sight. His appearance, I must admit, suggested the supernatural. He was tall; his long hair came down to his shoulders and his beard covered his chest. He had large blue eyes, placed in sunken sockets. One had the feeling, when he looked at you, that he was seeing through you.

It was those blue eyes and the lilt of his Irish voice what first attracted me to him – this when I was a schoolboy and I always had the subconscious urge to call him 'Sir'. He had long tapering fingers and his hands were not rough like other people's. We children were ordered to shun him as if he was the devil himself and we knew we were in for a good hiding if we were seen in his company.

One day I told him I had had a warming up for being with him.

'Never mind, laddie,' he said; 'stick your chin out and say, like I do: "Nil desperandum."' Someone gave me away and told my parents they had seen me talking to Jobey but before getting the usual punishment I was asked what he had told me. On my replying: 'Nil desperandum', I was given a double issue, one for disobeying and the other for using bad language in the home. When I mentioned this to Jobey some time afterwards, he told me he had known scores of boys punished for not knowing their Latin, but never a man.

As time passed away, I spent more time in his company. He taught me the names of a large number of stars in the sky and showed me how to find my way across the fens by fixing the Pole Star and the Plough. Shakespeare, Shelley and Byron he would recite to me. It was to him I owe my knowledge of Greek mythology and he would spend hours teaching me how to render first aid to the injured as only an expert could teach. He would have fits of depression, when he would drown his sorrows in a bottle of Irish whiskey and would sing the only song we ever heard him sing: 'Forty Years On'. During these bouts he would inform me that there was only one hall – Trinity Hall; that the Rotunda was the only hospital worthy of the name. To the drinking of the last drops in the bottle he would toast damnation to all females, then, falling into a drunken slumber would mutter about a man; a prayer; a bundle of rags and a hank of hair.

The only time I saw him angry was when I told him a child had died with diphtheria; had choked before the doctor arrived. 'Heavens above,' he shouted, 'is not my punishment finished yet?' One day an incident occurred which altered the attitude of the local people towards him. A man was using an axe when it slipped and bit deep into his leg. Jobey happened to be nearby and hearing shouts and screams went to see what it was all about. He calmly called for hot water and clean linen. He then astounded the onlookers by taking a metal case out of his pocket, and after tying up the severed artery, washing the wound and bandaging it, he sent the man straight off to the hospital.

On his return some time later, this man was loud in his praise of Jobey and announced to everyone that they had said at the hospital he was lucky to be alive. They also said that no doctor could have made a better job than Jobey did. This praise of his skill in first aid drove him again to the bottle and the song 'Forty Years On' again echoed across the fens, arousing the pity of the wife of the man whose life had been saved. She made him a pot of tea and with trembling limbs approached his door. Getting no reply, she walked in. This happened just as he was draining the last of the bottle, to the accompaniment of his usual feminine curse. Drunk as he was, Jobey, on seeing her, said, 'Madame, are you aware you are intruding. Will you please get outside?'

When I called in that evening, he told me he would have to give up the whiskey as he had been seeing things. From that time I never saw him again the worse for drink. People with sores and cuts used to come to him for treatment and one old man, who had given up work because of some internal disorder, was put back on his working feet as a result of medicine supplied by the chemist on the written instructions of Jobey. Little gifts of eggs, butter and other tit-bits would be left at his cottage. Contact with other people altered his habits; his hair and beard he had trimmed by one of the men and one day he asked me where was the nearest Roman Catholic church. On being told, he suggested we should walk there the next Sunday. We did so and he left me and entered the church. After a long wait, I was surprised to see him come out arm in arm with the priest.

During the long walk home, the only words he spoke were: 'Confession is good for the soul.' From that date he became very unsettled, until, one day, the priest drove over to see him, bringing a large parcel of clothing. On inquiring what was the idea, I was told he had a hankering to be off to the mountains of Mourne because he had a penance to perform and if he met a lady as he hoped, his pilgrimage would have been brought to a successful conclusion. A cab was coming in the morning to take him to the station. He unlocked his battered old trunk; took out a polished oak case, at the same time saying: 'I am now going to show you what only my eyes have looked on for the last five years.' On his lifting the lid, I saw a complete set of surgical instruments and as he said: 'Everyone silver-plated.' An inscribed plate on the lid read as follows: 'Presented to Professor [here the name was concealed by a strip of adhesive tape] Cantab. M.D. Edin. F.R.C.S Eng. F.R.S. – by past and present students of Dublin University Medical School, on the occasion of his marriage'

As he re-locked it back in the trunk, he remarked: 'That is a sure sign and proof of your old fen saying: Never give as a present

anything that cuts. It will only bring bad luck.' I bade him farewell and that was the last I saw of him.

A few weeks later I was surprised to receive a complete set of
Byron's works, bound in leather. Enclosed was this note: 'From
Jobey, the man who regained his self-respect whilst living in the
Norfolk Fens.' The post-mark was Dublin, December 1903.

EDWARD RIGBY, M.D., F.L.S.
1747–1821

Reference books will inform you about Edward Rigby's life as a doctor in the Norfolk and Norwich Hospital, but I have yet to come across one book which deals with the folk tales regarding his life at Framingham Earl. Local lore includes a lot of details regarding the things he did when living at the Old Hall. He not only ran a smallpox hospital there. He, being a man who believed that trees had life just like human beings, was in effect a tree worshipper. In furtherance of this cult, he turned people out of the cottages on his estate; pulled the houses down, then planted trees on the site. He was mayor of Norwich in 1805, and he used his office to persuade the corporation to plant lots of trees. Hence afterwards, years later, Norwich was named 'The City of Trees'.

Being accoucheur consultant at the hospital did not prevent him from doing his homework. He fathered twelve children, the last four being born at one birth, in 1817, when he was seventy and his wife forty. As a reward for this feat, Norwich Corporation presented him with a piece of silver plate. However, the quads lived only twelve weeks. He was a man who believed that what one has done once, one can do again. Accordingly he read up all the information he could obtain regarding the Hebrew prescription of the tonic Jacob used so that Leah could spend her time in raising stock instead of working in the fields. Although he failed to father more children after the quads, one must give him credit for the fact, that, by using the juice of the mandrake root as a go-getter, he laid the foundation for chemists to work, so that 150 years later, doctors were prescribing to childless wives, what is now known as the fertility pill.

Being also one who had faith that certain herbs played a great part in fighting the various diseases to which the human body was heir, he had a large plot in his garden devoted entirely to herb growing. By observation he made the discovery that the hordes of wild rabbits which bred at an enormous rate fed chiefly on wild sorrel. He cultivated a large patch of this herb, using it as a salad eaten with skate on meatless Fridays.

Edward Rigby also grew the wild white poppy, which was the source of his opium supply. Hemp provided him with a relief for chest complaints; its leaves being burnt in a saucer and the resulting smoke inhaled. Accordingly, it may well be believed that he must have had some use for deadly nightshade, also the black fungus called toadstools; both being lethal if eaten. He did build a loo for the house in a circle of evergreens. It had a wooden seat over a pit. All the rain water from the roofs were piped into this pit, which, after flushing, ran in earthenware pipes for over two hundred yards into a ditch. This ditch grew an abundance of water cress. It so happened that the doctor's wife was very fond of this water cress and, in spite of the richness of the mud in which the roots flourished, she lived to the age of ninety-five years.

Dr Rigby was seventy-four when he died. Being the squire of the parish, he was buried at the east end of Framingham Earl church; this being a spot usually reserved for the parsons in the churchyard. Massive tombs were erected over his and his family's graves. Sad to relate, these tombs today are nothing less than a heap of brick rubble. However, over the way in the nearby garden of the Old Hall, a mass of what was once garden herbs, now gone wild, keeps his memory green.

BAWBURGH'S TREASURE

The mentioning of the fact in the preceding tale of the custom of burying parsons on the east side of a church reminds me, in a roundabout way, of one relating to the pretty little village of Bawburgh, situated some four miles west of Norwich.

Like many other parishes, Bawburgh boasts a church, chapel, shops, public house, one-time grist mill, school, vicarage, a public telephone and a fair quota of council houses. There used to be a hall, built in 1634, but this was pulled down a few years ago. There was supposed to be a tunnel leading from that hall to a farmhouse, the other side of the river, which latter used to be the residence of priests. Still standing in the hall grounds are a dovecote and a refectory. At one time there was a hermit's lodge (we would today call it a guide's cottage) near the village bridge. This is still marked on Ordnance Survey maps with a cross. Some of the building materials can be seen incorporated in the walls of nearby cottages.

Until the enclosure in 1813, Bawburgh possessed Common Land. There were also two parish pits, of which one – a sand pit – remains (reminder of the days when the responsibility of the upkeep of the local roads rested on the local people; reminder too of the days when a simple floor covering of sand was the custom in cottages). Perhaps less common are the examples of prehistoric man – in the form of crude flint implements – found on the heathland to the north-west, known by the gruesome title of 'The Hangings'. Less common too is perhaps the discovery of a Roman cremation cemetery, in 1947.

There is, however, one thing in Bawburgh, the like of which it shares with just one other Norfolk parish. The object is the 'healing' well of St Walstan, situated in the orchard of that former priests' house, now known as Church Farm. So secluded is this that it is said that a number of parishioners are unaware of its exact whereabouts. It is on private property near and to the north of the ancient church of St Mary and St Walstan but readily recognizable by the comparatively modern square-shaped brick parapet which surrounds the shallow circular well itself and which is lined with, in the main, unfaced flint.

Like Walsingham, Bawburgh (or Babur as some of the older residents will still have it, meaning beautiful village), has been a place of pilgrimage for many centuries, in particular in this instance for the ailing or maimed. As a result of partaking the reputed healing waters of this near 1,000 years' well, many have claimed relief, although many people believe that the extent of the cure depended on the measure of faith which was put into this climax of pilgrimage. Indeed, during my own spell of living in the village – from 1935 until 1955 – I have had people call at my house asking for final directions to the place after having travelled as far as from the southern counties of England – just to take back bottles of the water.

Many were the cures effected – so we are told – and some miracles (according to the scribes whose writings revealed that their measure of faith equalled their oft vivid descriptions) resulted from external application of the healing water; this in addition to drinking it. There is one recorded instance relating to the morning of Saturday, 19 February 1842, when one Dame Mary Magdalen Mcdonnell, of the Hammersmith convent, 'fell ill September, 1841, with violent pains in her teeth and face, followed by cough, tenderness of the chest, slight spitting of blood, and other symptoms of consumption, which gradually increased, until she took to her bed entirely, December 17 1841.' On 17 February 1842, the lady was so ill that her death was expected in a matter of hours.

On 19 February however, an attempt to revive her with water brought from Bawburgh's Well proved so successful that two days later she was able to depart from her bed; this after she had 'slept seven hours on her left side, on which she had not been able to lie for months', and it is recorded that in 1858 the good lady still lived.

Yet another instance; this nearer home, at Wymondham. In 1787 there was born in that place a person called Francis Bunn. Joining the Militia in 1810, he was discharged five years later suffering from 'incurable' ulcers. Having married a Catholic when in Ireland before his discharge, he 'attended Mass with her, for the first time in his life, at Cossey Hall'. In 1818 the couple took up residence in Costessey (the present spelling), and in 1819, having heard of Bawburgh's miraculous well, he set out on a difficult three miles' tramp and in due course applied the water to the smitten leg. We are told that on the return journey he was able to discard his stick and that from the next day the wound caused no more trouble. In fact, 'Dr. Husenbeth declares that from 1820 he used from time to time examine Bunn's leg, and can attest the wound continued healed up to the time of Bunn's death in November, 1856.'

Much more recent is the instance whereby a patient in Norfolk and Norwich Hospital asked for and obtained a bottle of the well water before undergoing a serious operation. He was reported as making a wonderful recovery and was convinced he was assisted by the water.

What do we learn of the man, Walstan, from whom both the Well and the Church of Bawburgh take the name? Born at Bawburgh sometime between 960 and 970, he came of parents, Benedict and St Blide, of no mean wealth and rank. Some historians believe that one or the other was related to one of the Anglo-Saxon monarchs. They also believe that Walstan 'was nearly related to King Edward Ironside' who died in 1016 (the same year as Walstan's death). St Blide (the name is believed to be the forerunner of the Norfolk known name Blyth) is recorded as being buried in Martham Church.

Walstan had no desire for wealth and accordingly was quite

content working as labourer on a farm in Taverham, a village five
or so miles to the north of Bawburgh. Although receiving wages
just sufficient to support him, as a result of having made a life-
long agreement with the farmer, he still found ways, to his own
disadvantage, of assisting those in greater need than he. Incensed
at his giving away shoes she had given him because he was bare-
footed, the farmer's wife gave him what she thought to be an
almost impossible task. So surprised was she at his apparent
supernatural powers in successfully completing it, that she craved
forgiveness.

Later in life, as a measure of appreciation for the good work
Walstan had done, the farmer gave him a cart and the produce of
a cow about to calve. Two bull calves resulted.

A visitation affecting Walstan took place on 27 May 1016, and
his death three days later was foretold. True to foretelling, he
passed away in a field at Taverham on the 30 May, near the church
there. The need for water in connection with the administration of
the sacrament in his dying moments was met by the 'springing up'
of a well which was known as St Walstan's Well. It was in accord-
ance with his wishes that he should be put on his cart and buried
in the place where the cart, drawn by the two oxen – his oxen too
– finally rested.

A well marks the place where the oxen paused for rest on
Walstan's last earthly journey, also known as St Walstan's Well
(and shown on Ordnance Survey and other maps) and the beasts
finally came to rest at Bawburgh and the village thus became the
place of his burial.

The way to that last resting place at Bawburgh was through the
river Wensum and after going through the Cossey Woods and
through part of the park of the then Lord Stafford, the oxen
mounted a hill, then rested awhile. Here a second spring came
into being, also called St Walstan's Well, which, it is said, produced a steady flow of pure water. This lasted until the end of the
eighteenth century, when it dried up. However, of the three
springs, the one at Bawburgh is the only one to which miracles
have been ascribed.

The body of Walstan was enshrined in a chapel on the north
side of the church. Of that chapel nothing now remains, as it was

demolished in the reign of Henry VIII and plundered of its treasures. The sacred remains were burnt, together with relics of devoted pilgrims and the ashes thrown to the winds. Because there was now no support for the north wall of the church, this being situated on hilly ground, a large and somewhat ugly strengthening buttress was built, which can be seen to this day. It is said too that the oxen also drew the corpse through an opening especially made in the north wall of the church; this subsequently being blocked up. To this day too can be seen the outline of a large arch in that wall.

In olden days the pilgrims discarded their footware in the Slipper Chapel, were met by the hermit or guide near his abode by the bridge and escorted by him to the Well. Various attempts have been made during the present century to revive the pilgrimages. Perhaps the most recent attempt was the one in the early 1950s, when the village clergyman held a service there. Evergreen sprays were dipped into the water and splashed over the surrounding ring of participants.

There was a widespread belief in this part of Norfolk that the water of St Walstan's Well was highly effectual in curing the maladies of farm animals, and one Mr Sparrow who was an occupier of the Church Farm earlier in the present century, although a Protestant, shared the general conviction of his neighbours. At the same time he seemed to seek a natural rather than a supernatural solution to the attributed healing powers of the water 'of some mysterious mineral or vegetable substance no chemical analyst has been able to detect'. Nevertheless, sad to relate, it was not so many years ago that the local council did have the water analysed and as a result declared it unfit for human consumption.

Which reminds me again about the custom of burying parsons on the east side of a church. One exception is that the same clergyman who attempted pilgrimage revival is himself buried on the north side of Bawburgh Church – somewhere over the shrine of St Walstan, and, let it be added, his memorial is also there for all to see.

STONE COFFINS MAKE FINE PIG-FEEDING TROUGHS

More than sixty years ago, I was sent with a horse and cart to fetch a load of lime from a lime-kiln at West Dereham in south-west Norfolk. Arriving at the Kiln, I carried out my employer's instructions to unharness the horse and give it a feed. Then I set out to find the lime-burner, who I found was an aged man well over eighty; endowed with a wonderful memory and gifted in the art of folk-tale telling. Here is the story he related during his dinner hour break.

'This lime-kiln goes back to eleven hundred and eighty years. It was built to supply the mortar to build the abbey, whose ruins you can see in the corner of a field close by. In the year 1500, all the land around here was owned by Francis Dereham, who, I've been told, mucked about with his old sweetheart, Queen Katherine Howard, the wife of King Henry VIII. Queen Katherine was a warm bit of goods — I reckon she was born in a lime-kiln. However, one day Francis Dereham was caught with his trousers down and Katherine too with most of her clothes off. The King made sure that it would not happen again, by ordering Francis to be beheaded. His body was brought down here and buried in the abbey. His severed head was lost on the way from London to here, and any old folks will tell you that his ghost can be seen looking for his head in the abbey grounds. I myself have not seen it

96

because I never go out in the night, being aware that this area is one of the most haunted spots in Norfolk. Since then a lot of things have happened here. The King, on hearing that the monks at the Abbey were praying for the soul of Francis Dereham, sent some soldiers down, to turn the monks out of the Abbey. Before leaving, the soldiers raped nuns in the nearby convent and their screams can still be heard on a dark winter night. At least, old shepherds – being about at all hours of the night during the lambing period – swear they often hear it, but perhaps what they hear is the owls' hooting in the abbey ruins.

'But one thing about which I am sure is I spend most of my time on what at one period was holy ground, for I have to dig the chalk to burn into lime. This comes from what was once a burial ground hundreds of years ago. I don't dig up any bones, but those fat old monks were a lazy lot, because I find stone coffins only a couple of feet under the surface. It's a good many years ago when I found the first stone coffin, and my boss, who owned the land, said, "Just what I wanted. My old sow has chewed up her wooden trough, and she will get toothache if she starts biting stone." Someone told the parson the old sow was having her dinner served on a stone plate. He was in a furious temper; shouting that it was sacrilege placing the coffin in a sow's sty, and he went on rampting that all those coffins contained the remains of the virgin nuns who had died in the convent. I cut him short by saying that it was something worth knowing that there were virgins in the village, even if they were underground.

'Sometime afterwards the parson turned up again. With him was another parson who stated he was the Bishop of Ely and the patron of West Dereham living. The latter said I was to stop digging out the chalk because those coffins were laid in consecrated ground. I said perhaps you can tell me if that is the reason why chalk is so darned hard – that it wears the point of my pick out in less than a month. I was told the Bishop was not interested about that point and as he walked away I informed him I was, because the blacksmith charged me one shilling to re-point my pick.

'Things quietened down for a time. Then my boss died and his widow took over the lime-kiln. She still owns it and you will see her name is Mrs Harrisson, printed on the bill I will give you when I have loaded your lime. Well! to get on with my tale: one day a chap turned up and said he was a lawyer to the Bishop of Ely. I was told I would have to stop digging chalk and coffins. I replied, "You had better come along and see my missus, and I warn you, she has the gift of the gab which will beat any lawyers." So I took him to see her, and was leaving the lawyer with her when she said, "You stop here, Ben; I don't want to be left alone with this tricky gent." This because that lawyer had already started to read a paper he had in his hand, in which were instructions forbidding her to dig any further chalk. On hearing this she reared up and told him in real Norfolk style to hold his hosses and that she would show him something. She then produced the deeds which were drawn up when her late husband bought the land known as The Lime Kiln. She pointed out the clause which stated that the purchaser would have all timber and mineral rights. "Now, Mr Lawyer, how much will the Bishop of Ely give me to own these rights? I don't think he will buy at my price; I shall want thousands of pounds." That was the end of a fuddy-wuddy bishop's attempt to interfere in my getting an honest living.

'The parson turned up once again and as good as told me he was putting a curse on the chalk pit with book, bell and candle. But that was no worry to either my missus or me, because she was making a profit and I was making a living.' With those words the old man ended his tale.

Several years later than the old man's tale and during the First World War, I had a tent mate who came from West Dereham. One day I said to him: 'How is the stone coffin trade at your home?' 'Dead,' he replied, 'and so is the old lime-burner who sold them. They were bringers of ill luck. The last one was bought by a wealthy American who had it shipped to New York. He followed on the Titanic; on her first voyage, and when the ship went down, he went down with her.' On hearing this bit of news, I thought the parson's curse on the chalk pit had what we Norfolk folks termed as having plenty of stuffing behind it.

FERTILE SEED OF
ISHMAEL

Whoever wrote Genesis, the first chapter in the Bible, must have realized that he was preserving for posterity the first and greatest folklore tale ever published. As a student, self-taught, of the lives of all those mentioned in Genesis, I think: what a lusty crowd they must have been! My opinion is not based on the written word. It was made as a result of coming into contact with a man who claimed he could trace his ancestry right back through the ages, to the time when Abraham's wife, in a jealous rage, told him that unless he got rid of his private secretary and her baby, of which he was the father, she would be clearing out and taking his lawful heir with her. This upset Abraham, because his wife was a good cook, who could make the old crone ewes of his flock taste like young lamb. He also found in Hagar his home help a comfort to an old man who was fond of her baby; for not only had he circumcised that child, he had also chosen the name for it, which was Ishmael. So when Abraham saw his wife had started packing her clothes, he said to Hagar, 'The bottom of the trade has been reached in the sheep and goat market, so I am cutting down on my staff. You will have to find another job.' Hagar, being aware she was living in a tied tent, rather than be evicted, took Ishmael and wandered into the desert. Then, when the child started crying with hunger, she laid him down on 'the ground, and started

99

weeping herself. Although there was no one near, she heard a voice say, 'Why weepest thou?' As if talking to herself, she replied, 'Abraham, having had his way with me, has turned me out of his tent. Now I am an outcast wandering in the desert, with my baby dying of hunger and thirst.' 'Don't fret,' said the voice, 'your son Ishmael will live to be a very old man, and his descendants will become a great nation, spreading all over the world.' So ends the written tale.

I now go on to what Gipsy Gray told me. His mother was Queen of her tribe, who handed to her son the folk tale told from one generation to another, of how Ishmael married an Egyptian woman who bore him several sons, who, when they grew up, wandered all over the known world, buying up horses, which they sold to the King of Egypt. In the course of time, as the world grew larger, they became known as gipsies; whose tribe was founded by Ishmael in Egypt and, as the voice predicted to Hagar, they are now scattered all over the world. They are a dark-complexioned race, having no settled abode, but retaining the racial instinct which enables them to remain unbeaten as horse dealers. Having an international language of their own, they can wander around the world. Their women folk have the gift of foreseeing the future and they are also good mothers to their children.

Gipsy fathers are not interested in their children until they are grown up; due no doubt to the fact that the founder of gipsy tribes never knew his father. They have no so-called religious beliefs. Living from day to day, they do not worry about what happens after they have taken their last breaths. Also, as Gipsy Gray said, 'All we are sure about is that after we are buried, all our possessions are burnt by fire. There is no memorial of our life here on earth, yet we still retain the old Egyptian belief in re-incarnation, which was the faith of our forefathers.' He said, too, that when a gipsy died, and until a law forbade it, he had the right of burial in the place where he died. Generally the spot chosen for death was on a windswept heath, miles from the nearest habitation. His grave was a round hole, in which he was buried standing upright. When the hole was filled, it only covered a small space. On the surface were planted roots of bracken, and

FIG. 7.

in the course of a few weeks no one could tell the soil had been disturbed. There was no cant, nor mystic rites, when a gipsy was placed in the earth. A few words were spoken by the head of the tribe; the same as spoken thousands of years ago: 'Thou hast proved you were a true son of Ishmael. You have wandered afar and during your travels nearly every man's hand was against you and ready to strike you. Yet you have flourished. Now your spirit has gone to a far-off land and the places that have known you all your life will know you no more, ever. Even the place where you have been laid to rest will soon be forgotten.'

Gipsy Gray stated there was an exception to the last few words, for to this day a gipsy grave can be seen at Kenton, between Newmarket and Bury St Edmunds. A gipsy lad is buried there who was falsely accused of being a thief. This worried him until, broken-hearted, he ended his own life and, as was the custom of those days, he was buried in the centre of cross-roads. Up to this day, too, every true gipsy who passes by, places a few wild flowers on a piece of black cloth on his grave 'In remembrance'.

OLD SHUCK

Passing through the village of Salthouse on the north Norfolk coast, just over sixty years ago, I saw an aged man sunning himself outside the Dun Cow, into which I went for a drink; getting one too for the old man, whom I joined on his seat. 'Nice and warm in the sun', I said. 'It is today, but you want to be here in the winter when a Nor' Easter is blowing in from the sea. That's the time when this place is known as the Icehouse', he replied. I gathered his name was Sam Rudd and that he had lived in the village all his life; also, still got a fair living digging lug worms for bait.

He sat quiet for a short spell, then asked, 'Ever heard of Old Shuck, the ghost dog?' 'Yes, I have,' I said, 'but several places claim they have an Old Shuck.' 'They may do,' was his reply 'but there is only one ghost dog, and he is only seen between here and Cley-on-Sea. Now, sit quiet and I will tell you: I have not only seen him but I have had to run like hell when he chased me home one night.

'I had been bait-digging but just as dark was falling I had to give up as to the tide was rising fast. I started on my four miles' walk homewards along the beach, keeping a sharp look on the high tide mark to see what had washed up. That was in the days of sailing ships, and often drowned sailors from wrecks would be left high and dry when the tide turned. Sometimes I would find one. Sailors in those days wore gold rings on one finger. This I would remove; turn out his pockets. Anything there was mine. If he had come ashore in the parish of Salthouse, I would drag him back into the sea, knowing the ebbing tide would carry him out to sea where the current would carry him along, until he came ashore near Cromer. The reason for my doing this was, all washed-up dead sailors were buried by the parish in whose boundary they were found. It was all right for the parson, undertaker, and grave-digger, who each took their cut, but it was hard luck on us folks who had to find the poor rate levied by the churchwardens to pay for the burial, and beside this, Salthouse had only a small church-yard. Cromer had a large cemetery with plenty of room to plant those men who came in from the sea. I did not find anything that evening I am telling you about, and having reached the beach road which led to the village across the saltings, I clambered over the shingle bank and was no sooner on the road when a heavy sea mist came swirling down. A pitch black darkness set in. I did not worry because I knew by the feel of my feet if I stepped off the hard road.

'I then heard a dog howling and baying some distance behind me. It was so loud it drowned the roar of the sea pounding the shingle bank. I was wearing a pair of heavy thigh boots and after kicking them off I ran like a greyhound in my stockings. The faster I went, the nearer came the howling. At last I reached my home. I opened the door; entered, and bolted it as quickly as I could. My father was sitting in front of the fire, and he said, "Where are your thigh boots?" I told him not to worry about the sea boots; instead to listen to that big dog howling outside, which had nearly caught me.

'Father got up out of his chair; took his fowling gun off its hooks on the wall; put in the barrel a double charge of gunpowder; rammed it down with a wad of paper. He then put about half a pound of heavy lead shot on top, and having put a firing cap on the gun nipple, went upstairs; opened his window; saw the dog squatting on its haunches; took aim and fired – but it did not stop the dog howling. When father came downstairs he said, "I pumped half a pound of swan shot into that dog but did not knock it over; nor stop its howling. It's Old Shuck right enough and you were lucky to get indoors before he caught you."

'At break of dawn we went outside. There was no sign of a dog but the privy door some distance away was riddled with shot holes, which proved to father that heavy shot would go right through a ghost dog, just as water would run through a sieve.'

With these words the old chap stood up. 'Thanks for the drink,' he said. 'I have an order for five hundred lug worms, so I must get along bait-digging then get home before dark because I am nearly ninety and cannot run if Old Shuck chases me.'

On leaving the old chap I went on to Cley-on-Sea, calling on the rector there, the Reverend Everett James Bishop, who informed me that the story I had heard at Salthouse was a fairy tale put out by Cley fishermen, to ensure the locals kept indoors whilst they, the fishermen, were making a smuggling run. Being interested, I visited an old fisherman, who was also a wild-fowler, named Pinchen. He told me to pay no regard as to what the parson said because he had not been in the parish very long, and one had to have his roots in Cley for many years to understand its traditions and folk tales. He then remarked, 'I can tell you the story of Old Shuck from its beginning. Nearly two hundred years ago, a sailing ship was driven ashore during a fierce storm. Every one of the crew perished. The captain, seeing his ship was breaking up, grabbed his pet dog, a large wolf hound, by its collar, and leapt into the boiling breakers. The huge waves engulfed both man and dog. They were eventually washed ashore. The man still had his grip on the dog's collar, and the dog had his master's reefer jacket clamped in his jaws, as if he was supporting his master in trying to swim ashore. The man was buried in Salthouse church-yard. The dog was buried on the beach. Soon afterwards, people heard and saw a large dog howling and running and seeking its master. As years passed away, my great-grandfather, my grand-father, my father and I have both seen and heard the dog. Call me a liar, if you feel so inclined, but, having spent a good many years on the sea, I can only tell you: there are many things on this earth we fail to understand and Old Shuck is one of them.'

BEAK AND CLAW JUSTICE

I suppose it was one of the largest rookeries in the country. One can understand how that large wood came by the name 'Crow Hall', because in early spring hundreds of rooks – or crows, some called them – built their nests and reared their young ones. From dawn to dusk there was a terrible din of Caw! Caw! from the tree tops where the nests were built close together which enabled the rooks, chummy birds as they were, to gossip with each other as they carried on with family duties. If it was windy weather the nests would sway backwards and forwards. Children passing along the edge of the wood would pause and watch, shouting out a jingle youngsters had repeated down the ages:

> Rock-a-bye baby in the tree tops,
> When the wind blows the cradle will rock,
> If the bough breaks the cradle will fall,
> And down will fall baby and cradle and all.

This often happened in a gale, for the nests were only bundles of twigs. Nature in its wisdom had endowed the rooks with the knowledge that open-work nests discouraged the fleas, a pest from which the birds suffered. Young birds at times would be thrown from the nests and the old ones, instead of flying down to help, would soar up and up until they were mere specks in the sky, shortly after this where necessary re-build nests and if not too late in the season make preparations to rear successive families.

One thing over which country folk pondered was how did the rooks know the exact time of sunset because as the sun went down they would all leave the nests, fly to a large meadow where they would crowd together, strut about and caw away in chorus. The noise would then stop and after a brief silence they would take off in the fading light and return to their nests to settle down for the night. This performance would be pointed out to children, the interpretation being that the rooks never went to bed without saying their prayers, for grown-ups firmly believed that was what the rooks were doing in that meadow; a kind of bird evensong of thanksgiving for having survived another day.

I started studying rooks' habits at quite an early age, when, as a crow scarer, I earnt my bread and butter stopping those birds pinching the corn seed in a newly sown field adjoining the Crow Hall wood. I had to be on the job as the first streaks of dawn appeared in the sky. I would be on the run from one end of the field to the other, for the birds were in a hurry to give the young ones breakfast and I could only suppose they thought that field of new sown corn was a direct answer to their prayer of the previous day. Having made a mass attack and failed to obtain the breakfast cereal, they would split up into small parties and whilst I was busy scaring one lot off, others would be busy a short distance away. It was warm work for a time, until the plough teams appeared. The birds would then fly off to other sources for their food and the rest of their breakfast would consist of grubs and wire-worm. I, in turn, would have a restful time for the rest of the day.

One day, when there was more noise than usual in the tree tops, I wondered what was upsetting the birds. They would soar up in the air one second, then back to the nests in another. They kept this up for quite a long time. It seemed the whole rookery was boiling with excitement. Then something happened which if I had not seen it I would not have believed it. The whole flock of birds flew to the meadow, with one exception: a solitary rook remained, perched high on the topmost branch of a tree. As I watched and listened to them strutting up and down cawing to each other, I was amazed to see another flock of rooks, whose nests were in a second wood two miles away, fly in and join in the noise the others had been making. There must have been a lot of speech-making because they kept it up for over an hour. Then the whole lot rose, making a spiral climb until one could hardly see them, so high were they in the sky. Suddenly they all made a flying dive until they were just above the lone rook; circling around and making a terrible racket with their cawing. Two birds then detached themselves from the flock and persistently tried to knock the lone one off his perch. For a while he resisted their attacks but at last he was compelled to take wing. He tried to fly away but once he was in the air he was surrounded by the whole flock, each one trying to get a peck at his head. At last he fell; only a few yards from where I was standing. I picked him up. He was dead. The top of his head was smashed, caused by the powerful jabs from his fellow rooks' beaks. On seeing his breast feathers matted with egg yolk I was aware he had been caught in the act of robbing other nests of their eggs. For this crime he had to pay the penalty laid down by that age-long law, that if a member of a flock robbed other members he was to be tried and sentenced to death.

At sunset the rooks were much quieter than usual and I fancied they were tired out after spending most of the day at a sitting of a Beak and Claw session, trying one of their kind.

LEARNING
THE HARD WAY

Beak and claw justice undoubtedly indicates that birds sport an element of common sense. Not all, however. I knew of one bird which had to learn the hard way. It is known that toads, slugs, wasps and mice can be included in an enemies-of-bees list but until a few years ago I had not included the blackbird in a similar category.

As was my normal daily custom, early each day I visited the top-of-the-garden apiary and I well recall the beautiful early May morning – it being 6.30. A few bees were taking advantage of the fine morning for an early foraging start; birds were singing in the nearby trees; high in the heavens a lark was both seen and heard; nearer, but a few feet from the observer and less than one foot from one of the hives, a fully-fledged blackbird, apparently oblivious to all activities going on around, was busily scratching itself.

Later in the day the same visiting routine was repeated. Again, in the same place, was that blackbird. This time he was in an alert attitude and again, oblivious to the observer, was watching the hive entrance, from which a strong force of bees was issuing and returning. Almost before it was realized what was happening, that cunning bird had made a dart at the immediate entrance and as quickly retreated to a nearby open space. Without wasting time a live bee was being dissected and in part forming a meal for this feathered robber. Four times within the next five minutes the sequence was repeated. This could be a serious matter – four foraging bees lost in five minutes. Instantly it brought to mind an instance of another blackbird, caught in the wire-netting cage of a soft-fruit garden, which was found to have just over one hundred and forty blackcurrants in its crop. However, less than the time it had taken to collect one's thoughts, the bird had almost completed the fifth round. This time the bees met him and he beat a hasty retreat – empty-beaked, so to speak.

More successful was the sixth journey. Then, on the seventh one, it happened. At the entrance a cloud of bees – at least that was what it looked like – met him angrily and attacked with such effect that he retired to of all places the place where he was originally seen. He then started to scratch himself in several different places in quick succession with a vigour which can best be imagined. From there he very soon flew, but not so fast, to a nearby woodpile; eventually lapsing into a haunched-up dejected position.

For several minutes that bird sat motionless. Then, out of the blue came the call of what must have been one of the elders of the blackbird tribe. It was answered by him flying – a bit more briskly this time after his rest – into the cooler atmosphere, in more ways than one, of the ivy-clad hedge.

Truly an instance of learning the hard way.

PART II

NOTES AND STORIES, TAPE RECORDINGS, FROM DIARY OF VISITS TO W. H. BARRETT

My first meeting with Mr W. H. Barrett resulted from my reading one of his books – *A Fenman's Story* – and, surprisingly to me, because I habitually jot such things down, I cannot recall the actual date. Nevertheless, I do remember it was a fine late summer evening when I arrived in the beautiful village of Framingham Pigot; a village I of course knew so well from early cricketing days on the park and the even earlier living in the adjoining village of Framingham Earl. I did not know precisely, however, where his home, Corner House, was, and towards this end asked someone trimming his roadside hedge, who indirectly answered, 'What, 's he still alive; he's been ill, hasn't he?'; which indicates that even a village 'grapevine' doesn't always flourish.

I knocked at the door, was soon confronted by Mrs Barrett, who after learning of my desire to meet the man who wrote such an interesting book, invited this stranger in. Within five minutes I was very much at home, because in that time I had replaced an electric light bulb, which for some unknown reason had fallen out of its socket overhead on to my shoulder; written down the reason for my visit on the (as I afterwards found) ever-ready note pad; started sipping a glass of wine. After a pleasant hour I bade goodbye and took my leave, to the accompaniment of an invitation to come again.

Although I note I paid four visits to Corner House after that (during one of which visits I returned a clock I had repaired for Mr and Mrs W. H.) it was not until the 29 November that I actually tape-recorded the promised story, or rather, stories, as it turned out to be. After setting up the recorder in a not too conspicuous place, the same for the microphone on its stand but near enough to the subject without dominating too much, a preliminary utterance from W. H. to get the recording level satisfactorily set, with all comfortably seated in front of a roaring fire and with Mrs Barrett an interested spectator, he began:

'When I look back after a long life and when I listen in to the wireless or to the television and I see the fiddlers busy at work, and when I seeing them putting their hands up their sleeves and getting their handkerchieves out and wiping the sweat off their brows, my mind goes back to the old days, when an old gipsy would sit on an up-turned beer barrel, and he would play for hours for the people to dance. He would never have a drop of sweat to wipe off for the simple reason every one was so pleased with his playing that they kept him well supplied with liquid refreshment.

'Well! do you know? That old man would make the violin talk and as you listened to him playing you could only visualize that he was a-playing something that had happened during his life-time in his family. Each tune he played had its own name. Well! he had that violin that was handed down from grandfather to grandchild. The only thing, he said, that wanted renewing, was the strings. He said that the old frame of the fiddle was as good then as it was the day it was made. Well! he happened to let me have a look at it. You couldn't tell what the wood was because age had darkened it, but there it was in plain letters: 1671; and that had been handed down, travelled thousands of miles in caravans. Of course he didn't do badly out of it; he kept on a flat piece of ground; sitting all by himself, and he'd strike up. Before long all the lads and lassies in the district within hearing distance came flocking up. And there they were, weaving, twisting; living in a land beyond all hardship of their ordinary life.

'He was an uncouth old chap; you'd have to be careful because he chewed tobacco and he had a habit of picking a target and if you didn't see it coming, well, you got it, but everybody liked the old chap. I spent practically six weeks with him; he'd broken his leg, and he had to lay in the bunk at the back of the caravan. Well! I was only a boy at the time, but the tales he told me were of his wanderings about the country. His parents brought him from Hungary and he travelled all the way round, and his fiddle was his living. He said he never wanted for a drink. He'd only got to go in a pub and give a few scrapes and the landlord would bring 'im a drink; send word round that the old fiddler had come; would they care to do a dance? He attended all fairs; didn't know a word of music. If you put a sheet of music in front of him, that was trying to tell a pig about Sunday. He didn't understand a note. What he understood was music, pure and simple, as it was in the days of Adam and Eve, when they danced round the apple tree. He had no tuition. I've heard, during my life-time, a lot of wonderful violins, players, but I've NEVER heard one that had such appeal as the old gipsy; and, as I've said before, the violin not only made music, it brought back history of suffering and all the cares of this world. Somehow or other he had the power of putting over just what his old tribe had suffered during their long trek from Hungary to Norfolk.

'He wasn't what you'd call a heavy drinker, but they always said he'd got to have seven pints before he could start playing, and he would not play unless there was an upturned beer barrel for him to sit on, because, he said, that gave him the power to work the strings.

'Well! he, like everybody else, reached the end of his life, and I can see him now, laying in the bunk at the dark end of the caravan, sawing away, sawing away, and the people used to stand outside, listening to him playing.

'Somehow or the other, he lost his fiddle. No one knew what had happened to it, but the old boy was going fast and his wife had several people in to see him. The last words he said were, "I've lost my old fiddle." No one knew for a long while what had happened to it, and then it was divulged (where it was). He was dying and his wife said that he'd had the violin all his life and his ancestors before him. He was the last of the line. She asked the man who kept the Ship Inn at Brandon Creek if he'd do her a kindness. So he said, "I will if I can; what is it?" She said, "Will you get a little bit of straw, and put my old man's violin on top of it and set fire to it?" "I don't want no one else, nor did he, to handle it." So the man set fire to it on a slab of stone – and the ashes were placed in the old gipsy's coffin. As the old lady said: "Don't matter where he was, he'd have his old fiddle with him."'

'That was quite a different story to the one about a man I knew when I was a youth. He was a rough old diamond, but he had a wonderful gift for music. Every Sunday afternoon people would see him walking down the streets of Littleport in Cambridgeshire. They'd say, "Hello, Mister!" "What, are you off again!", they used to say. "Yep, I'm going to fiddle the buggers to Hell." He was playing at the PSA (Pleasant Sunday Afternoon) at the Primitive Methodist Chapel. He had no religion, but he liked playing.

'Leaving violins a' one side; let's get back to bugles. There was a missioner who came down to hold a revival service, and that was the year Halley's Comet [4 May 1910] was seen. Well! us kids used to watch that comet; it had a tail hanging from it. This missioner, at the revival service, put the wind up everybody and said when that tail came off it would be the end of the world. We all stood out at the open-air meeting watching it, some young lads from Cambridge camping. The missioner didn't like the look of them because it was Sunday and they had been fishing. He gave them a real drumming down, then asked what would happen to them if they fell in the river? "Swim the other side." "Ah!", said the missioner. "The next time the world is destroyed that'll be by fire; where will you be then?" Back came the answer: "With the fire brigade." Well! the old man worked his congregation up with what would happen at the end of the world. They then dispersed and went home.

'The university lads thought they'd have a bit of fun because the old chap had told them what would happen when the trumpets sounded and the thunderstorms came back. So when all the local people were abed going to sleep there were the trumpets. These lads had got calls of the British Army; they'd put them on a phonograph, and over the fens came the calls. Everybody woke up. Fireworks went off. They were the explosions of the earth being rent in twain. At the same time the lads started banging and shouting. We lived in a double-dweller cottage and the partition between us and the neighbour was very thin woodwork, and as I lay in bed I heard the old man next door a-shouting "Here I am Lord; I'm waiting for yer. You'll know my house; that's the only house that's got the chimney pot. Oh Lord, dew come quick."

'Everyone got up. Then all of a sudden there was a big bang as a firework was let off, and they heard voices singing in the sky – the Heavenly Choir. They'd put a record on and the playing of it echoed over the fen. Well! the next morning – this was on the Sunday night – half of the people were at the Chapel before daylight; the other half was at the pub, waiting for it to open. They'd had such a sleepless night they wanted consolation. It was a long while before it came out that what people thought was the Last Trumpet was simply "Come to the Cook-house Door, Boys; Come to the Cook-house Door".'

'They called them the "Good Old Days". Of course, only ignorant people thought that. Just you imagine, a boy, eleven or twelve years of age, getting up in the morning; walking three miles to where the threshing tackle was. He'd be at work in the dust and that, all day. What did he get? Four pence a day. If you see any old photographs of threshing tackle, you'll see there is generally the beer bottle well in the foreground. Well! that beer bottle earned the boy more than he earned in wages, because the stacks were full of rats and the farmers always paid a penny a tail, for every tail handed in. The men used to take it out in beer. All the money collected was put in what they called the beer bottle. The boys used to take theirs out in cash. A boy's weekly wage was two bob a week. Very often he'd earned three-and-six or four bob a week rat-tail money, because the stacks were smothered with rats and it paid them to kill 'em. Well! there were only a few of them to share it.

'The old chap who fed the threshing machine had cut off the tails with his pocket knife; a few seconds later he'd open his dinner basket; pull out his bread-and-cheese and that; out with his pocket knife, and Ha! ha! ha! But it was all killing work. You see, a man never got a full wage of two shillings a day until he could carry corn all day. That was, carrying an eighteen (stones) sack of corn from the threshing tackle to the barn. Till he could do that he'd have one day trying of it. See? A lad of seventeen was classed as a three-quarter man. He got eight shillings a week. Well! to prove he was a three-quarter man, he'd have to spend all day, from half-past six in the morning till half-past five at night, carrying sacks of oats from the threshing machine — about a hundred yards — to the barn. Those sacks weighed twelve stones. I know what I'm talking about, because I've done the damn thing. Yes; and, I got my 'O' Level for it — education — and I was awarded eight shillings a week. But when I came to sit for the Higher Level or stand for the Higher Level, I only had one hour a-carrying eighteen stones a hundred yards before I packed in. I said, rather than have two shillings a day, I'd tramp the bloody roads, putting the gravel down that the farmers' carts had churned up. Just you imagine, a boy of today, at eleven years of age, getting hold of a horse's collar, with his plough harness, climbing into the manger because the horse used to hold his head up and he couldn't reach it. He'd push the collar over the horse's head; swing it round, and then take two of them out; to take his place as third ploughman. There was the head horseman; the second horseman; and the boy was third. He had to learn ploughing. Well! that meant that when turning round at the headlands, he would have to put the plough above his head to turn it round — he was so small. Yet he would have to plough his acre just the same as a man; one acre a day. In these days of mathematics, when every child is very clever, they couldn't come up to the old men, because, they would step out a field in yards, and, they'd get to within six inches of an acre. Where I was brought up there wasn't a field on that whole estate but what I could tell her how many yards to the acre, through stepping it out.

'They not only had to plough an acre a day; they also had to drill — when they had the first horse drills — they had to drill ten acres a day. A man used to have to hand hoe it them days. To earn a half-a-crown he'd have to hoe an acre, and that meant a-going for all he was worth from half-past six in the morning till half-past five at night.

'The hell of the life was the harvest. You'd see some lovely paintings of men at harvest. Well! I was sixteen when I was told I had got to do me harvest, with the other men. Well! that meant an outlay. I had to buy a scythe. Then I had to buy a "tommy-hawk"– to rake the corn in. On top of that, I had to buy a beer bottle. No man could harvest unless he had a gallon of beer a day. The brewers used to come round at a cheap rate: nine gallons for four-and-six, paid for after harvest. That was a special harvest brew, and I don't mind telling you if that brew was brewed today and they gave a man a breathing test, that 'ud bust the ruddy bag.

'You'd start mowing at half-past six in the morning. You'd wipe the last lot of sweat off about half-past eight at night. And how much do you think you would earn? Five shillings. That was ten shillings an acre. Well! after you'd mown, you'd got to tie it up in sheaves; then set it up in shocks. In those days every man wore two pairs of trousers; one back to the front, because they'd wear out the knees in a couple of days. It were the first three days which were hell. After that your muscles got used to it. I seen a strong man stand up and howl like a child, especially if there were a lot of green stuff in the corn that made it harder. See? Clean corn was all right, because your scythe would go through it, but if there was a lot of bindweed or scratch weed, that was like pulling a truck off a railway line. Once your muscles got used to it, it was nothing. What would a man say today if he was at work in the harvest field and his wife came along with a big bottle of white oils – horse oils; a shilling a pint from the chemist's. She'd come along and rub his loins, because he was in such agony. And when they talk of the "Good old days" . . . . Of course, I'll admit I was on the last lap of them. Things soon altered. When I see a man on his behind now on a tractor . . . still, there is a lot to be thankful for. When I smell the smoke, the hot oil and all the other sounds which went with it, I go back to the old times.' Mr Barrett concluded 'Speaking of people visiting traction rallies, if a man paid half-a-crown to go and see a traction engine at work when I was a boy, they would have shut him up.'

. . . . .

Apart from the folklore book, Jack, in talkative mood, told me stories connected with his earlier days. (How I wish the tape recorder was helping me to remember all he told me.) How, for instance, his father came in unexpected contact with a member of the Royal Family – with advantageous result to himself. Mr Barrett senior seemed to be able to turn his hand to anything in the woodwork line. He once had the job of replacing some worm-eaten panels in a well-known building in Ely. For some time before fixing them he worked on the major part at his home workshop. On the day he went to do the final fixing he took Jack – who was about five years at the time – with him. Following the train journey on the Downham Market, Southery, Littleport line, he worked on the oak panels; had just about finished in the late afternoon; was standing back, perhaps to admire, perhaps to cast a critical craftsman's eye, when a man came in and also examined the handiwork. Said he, 'I can't see which is the new; which is the old.' This observation was of course the ultimate praise which could be bestowed on a restorer of old things, and to show his appreciation he slipped a golden sovereign into the happy craftsman's hand.

It so happened that the train had to stop at one of the stations on the way home. One of the carriages – a saloon – was a royal one. Out of this stepped King Edward VII, to stretch his legs. The other waiting passengers did not take much heed of this because, in contrast to the custom of the gauntlet of sightseers which often present-day royalty have to run, they regarded him as just a good country squire. The King sauntered along the platform, passing a word here and there. He paused for a moment before Mr Barrett senior and said, 'You look very pleased, my man.' 'Yes sir, I have good reason for being so; I happen to have a picture of your mother in my pocket.' 'May I see it?' Mr Barrett pulled out the sovereign; told the story of the gaining of it. The King nodded his approval, turned to a member of his accompanying party and said, 'Give him another to keep it company.' The action was suited.

Mrs Barrett put some silver birch logs on to the now-waning fire – too good a wood to be burnt, I thought – and very soon the flames percolated their way through. Glasses of beer for two; a peeled apple for the third; a meditating lull in the conversation as each person weaved his and her own fantasies on the ever-changing flame patterns as the flames in turn weaved their up-the-chimney course.

PART III

REST OF THE TALES, GLEANED FROM MATERIAL OBTAINED FROM ANNE BARRETT

GOING TO BUNGAY

'As a child the answer I was given when I questioned an adult as to where they were a-gaining was "Oh Bungay". Old enough later to read a map I found it was the other side of the county, a long way from the fens. It was a great problem to me, how they got there and why they went so often. I was fifty years trying to solve it.

'Feltwell Fens where I lived was, in the winter, the last place created so the old men used to say, Slurk and Slub. From Brandon Creek to Hockwold cum Wilton, not a firm groundsel to place your feet, the whole weary miles. What were the people like, that lived in such a place? Some were the last of the old type of fenmen, dying out. Part modern fen drainage and the School Board Act were killing them. What men they were. Beer, bread and bacon had produced a race who in pubs, poaching and punting were more than experts, and what a mixture of blood ran in their veins, Saxon, Dane, Norman, with a dash of monks thrown in, for where else were the wayward brethren to go. After the abbot at Ely abbey had given them their cards and told them to find another job, only the fens could offer them sanctuary, it was a haven of refuge.

'Freedom and liberty ruled the lives of the old fenmen. A proof of this occurred when the police were searching the fens for Tug Mutton. Wanted on a charge for murder, even fifty years ago, some of us lads were listening to a group of our elders discussing as to where he could be hiding. One lad full of importance said, "I seed old Tug Mutton go down Sedge fen drove larst night." One of the men grabbed him by the neck, saying, "What you seed you seed, but keep your trap shut or you will get such a ding on the lug you won't forget for twenty Southery fearts." Same evening I heard an old man say, "There has been today as many policemen in Feltwell fen as there are fleas on my old dawgs back. And like those little old fleas, they have been running about all day and got nothing." Blessed with a sense of humour, they could always see the funny side. This is the way one of them told of his encounter with a gamekeeper. "I had jest snared a couple of long tails when I was chased by old velveteen and buttons. Seeing he could not run me down, he shouted, 'Stop or ille shute.' I said, 'Shute you dodman, but if you carnt shute better than you can run you couldn't hit a skept if it was tied on the barrel of your gun.'"

'Each fenman owned a pair of pattens. During a sharp spell they would skate miles over the fen rivers. Matches would be arranged and a lot of money would change hands in bets. They will never forget that match for the women's championship of the fens in the nineties. The favourite who was carr(y)ing a lot of money put on by the locals, came skimming down the course, well ahead of all the others. Suddenly she began to slow down. Some of her undies were slipping. Her father seeing what was happening and having a lot of money on his daughter, cupped his hands to his mouth and shouted, "Keep going Susan, you never wore none till you went to service." A kick and a shake and Susan won.

'There was another type of fenman – one-hoss farmers we called them – men who farmed as much land as only required one horse and man to work it. Most of these were thrifty, hard-working, God-fearing people, who for six days worked hard on the land and spent most of the seventh in the chapel, where now and again they would have revival services. Some of the older type attracted by the ringing would go too, fall under the mystic spell, turn over a new leaf, go off the beer, stop welting their wife and let the cock pheasant sleep in peace; then after a month or so, have a whole day on the booze, go home, tiddle up his family, and later get crossed off the chapel book as a total loss. So now you know where those gentlemen in Surrey Street got those last two words from.

'But the cream of the fens was the farm worker. He knew all there was to know about his job. To strangers he appeared sullen. It was not so. It was reserve, and once this was broken and you received an invitation to enter his home and try a glass of his home-made mead, you were treated as a brother. If he had any-thing to sell he would ask you what it was worth; the price you offered he would accept, expecting to get full value. When buying, it was the same. This simple faith in human nature was quickly discovered by the travelling tally man who accrued great profit as he went on his weekly rounds, happy as a bug on a baby.

'Not having had much schooling, books were not of great interest. He possessed two; a bible, his knowledge of which was obvious to all he came into contact with, and *Old Moore's Almanack* which gave him the phases of the moon and timetable of high water at King's Lynn, vital information to one living in constant fear of burst banks and flooded fen. A staunch liberal, in his view Cromwell was the greatest man in history and Gladstone was his prophet.

Dressed in mole skin trousers, blue gansy, a sleeved waistcoat and broad brimmed soft crown felt hat, with his frail (basket) and croome, he would walk miles to his work. If the job was not quite finished at the accustomed time of leaving off he would stop and finish it, no thought of extra pay; he would tell you, "My master treats me fair, so I try to do my best by him, and there I leave him."

'As a young man I was never up to a sight in the fens, so I moved out. After wandering around I settled down in the Reedham area. The first man I came into contact with was not a real fenman, but he had lived in the district long enough to acquire the charm of one. Beet bulbs and bees were his living and recreation. Others I soon met. I felt at home. I heard the same words and drawling speech. Things were done in the same way as they were done when I was a boy and, to crown all, a lady offered me a glass of bee wine. One sip proved it was the mead of the fens. With her "fare you well" ringing in my ears, I made my way home. At Berny Arms I saw a man crossing the marsh, his frail and croome on his shoulder. The old mill at Ashtree farm was in full sail, just as I had seen them working years ago, a sight that would have gladdened the heart of my old grandfather, the very last mill-wright of the now defunct Bedford level; they call it the catchment board now. There I was, miles away from where I had seen it all before. I could not sort it out. Same people, same speech, yet as I have said before, a sense of home. I left it at that.

'Later on at Norwich bus station, going into the room where you have to go when you want to ask questions, I said to the young woman that was sitting behind the table, "How do I git to so and so." "Go to Bungay", was her reply. Now I had not been told for such a long time to go to that old place so I got a bit riled, so I ups at her: "Look her young mawther, I asked you a civil question and dang it I expected a civil answer." "And I gave you one", she said. "Go to Bungay". I had heard before that it was no good trying to argue with a Norwich woman, so I went outside. A lot of buses were standing there. One of the drivers looked a chummy sort of chap so I asked him where he was a-going to. "Oh Bungay", he said. "All right wait a bit and I will go with you", and I jumped on the bus.

'After a little while, a chap comes along for the money, asking me where I was a-going. "Oh Bungay," I said. He wanted to know then whether single or return. Neither I told him. I was an old married man. It came to me afterwards what he meant was, did I want to go to Bungay alone, or a-go to Bungay and a-been to Bungay together. A working of all this out put me into a proper dither and when the bus stopped because there was a lot of water on the road, I did not know where I was, so I got off. There was a chap standing near in a blue gansy and bell-bottomed trousers, so I asked him where I was. "Oh Bungay, my beauty, have you come to see the floods." I gazed around and as far as I could see, water everywhere. I was back again in the fens and the reason of all the goes to Bungay that I had heard was plain before my eyes. Just take a glance at Samuel Woodward's map of Roman Norfolk. There you will see a stretch of blue water from Reedham. marshes to Feltwell fen. Now what was to prevent the lads and lasses from both those places in those days a-putting on their pattens, skimming over the ice, meeting at Bungay and over a horn of mead at the Boadicea Arms, making dates to meet again, until as usually happens in such circumstances, the lads from the west, skating on thin ice, went home with the girl from the east, and lived there happy till the end of his life.

'It is quite possible that my old Saxon ancestor in Feltwell fen, marrying the buxom skating partner his son had brought home from the Reedham marshes, put(ting) down his gotch after drinking the new bride's health, asking his son, "Where did you pick her up?" got the answer that was to puzzle the children for the next thousand years, "Oh Bungay".'

HOSPITAL PATIENT –
1913 STYLE

It was early in January 1913 that a patient arrived at the hospital in Kelling, Norfolk. He was one of the earliest to be given treatment under the Norfolk Insurance Committee that had just been set up. This patient, after being passed from one doctor to another, was finally told by one Dr Nash, the Medical Officer of Health for Norfolk, that a bed was being reserved for him at Kelling Sanatorium.

He will never forget that journey from Holt Station. The cab, provided by the local jobmaster, was an ancient contraption used only for one purpose – to carry patients to and from the sanatorium. On this journey the 'fare' inside, having had a long rail journey and his feet being cold, stamped them on the floor. Result – the bottom of the cab fell out and he had to run inside the cab until the approach to the railway bridge compelled the cab horse to slacken. The rest of the journey was completed up on the box beside the 'cabby' (who, by the way, did not give any rebate on this fare).

Kelling in those days consisted of three blocks: north and south wings for male patients and a women's wing. Seventy beds were the limit, some reserved for paying patients. The new patient was conducted to the north wing. This consisted of a block of low buildings called cubicles, very much resembling the stables on a stud farm. The difference was that the cubicle doors were never shut – wind, rain, snow drove in. This was his first introduction to fresh air treatment. Patients who had been there some time were quick to inform the new one that it was bitterly cold there and that the treatment was kill or cure.

Night nurse took your temperature at 6.30 a.m., then you went to wash and shave in an open shed in the north wing. Afterwards you made your bed. Four to six blankets were its covering; these and a large stone hot-water bottle were your only comfort. Catering was based on the system of what you had on the first Monday of the year, you would get for the next fifty-one Mondays, and so on. One bright patient would offer 25 to 1 on what you would have on any given day in three months' time.

Patients were supposed to do a certain amount of work, which consisted of from one hour cleaning brasses to six hours in the gravel pit. Those not working were supposed to take an hour's exercise along the Cromer road; women in the morning, men in the afternoon. The rest of the time, they had to sit in the shelters, just resting. Every patient had to rest an hour before meals and one after, just resting with no reading or anything allowed. This period was ushered in by a nurse running round ringing a bell and calling out: 'Legs up.'

No work was done on Saturday afternoons. This was when the workers had exercise and for most of them it was a hike to Bodham White Hart, the only pub within walking distance that would serve you. In those days the people of Holt were not keen on the sanatorium.

Sunday was visiting day, but very few visitors came. Everyone was too far from home. The Midland and Great Northern Railway did not run trains on a Sunday and buses were a thing of the future. At that time the sabbath at Kelling was dismal. One looked forward to bedtime on a Sunday; with hot bottle filled and snug beneath the blankets, you dreamed of the cosy home to which you were hoping to go back.

Thursday night was weigh night for all the patients who were up. Matron was clerk of the scales and if one had lost a little weight an extra dollop of porridge was awarded you. It was on the result of this weigh-in that you were graded in the amount of work to be done; if you gained weight you were given more work. It was a bit of a farce, for if a patient had the idea he had lost half a pound, he knew he would get a wigging from Matron. So into his pocket would go a pound or so of lead, handed from patient to patient.

On the whole the patients were a jolly set of chaps. It was truly a case of all being in the same boat and very rarely did one rock it. Some would get better and go home – to the same conditions they had left – generally carry on for a time then break down again. Others did not go home. Those who did best were those who made the most of a bad job, carried out the treatment and hoped for the best. Generally these were the type who at the end of their treatment walked to the station and pocketed the one-and-six-pence that was given for the cab fare.

The medical and nursing staff were of the stuff that heroes are made. They might be blue with cold, chilled to the bone, yet were always smiling and cheerful. The pay might be poor but they put everything into the job in hand. Each nurse was a real lady of the lamp, for on night duty they carried a lantern with a candle in it. As the years pass, my admiration grows greater, for with all the discomfort and grouses involved, by their skill and care they put me on my feet again to take my place in the outside world.

As one of the oldest ex-patients he earnestly asks all present and future patients at this hospital never to forget: 'It's thank God for the Friends of Kelling'

PART IV

ANNE BARRETT –
LIFE-LONG NURSE

ANNE – THE NURSE

Daughter of a railway station master, Anne Adela Mary Jones, as she was then, undertook training for nursing and did indeed obtain her nursing qualifications as long ago as 1912. Young as she was, work in hospital during the First World War, during which at times she was in charge of patients numbering over three figures because of the calls of more senior nursing staff elsewhere, proved a good training ground for that ever-desired attainment – experience.

By 1921 midwifery qualifications had been added. Then came her appointment as district nurse and midwife in Essex; this in fact covering a large rural area. No cars for nurses in those days. Distances too great for travel on foot were covered with the indispensable bicycle; on which, too, had to be carried the sundry medical equipment for non-emergency and, more often, emergency cases. In spite of long hours – often long hours away from home at that – cycling to and from 'cases' at varying times of day and night in all kinds of weather, there were rewards in the shape of gratitude of patients. Inevitably, there were heartbreaks too. Perhaps Anne Barrett's greatest at the time – she was married in 1917 – was the personal one. Out one day in 1924, she found on her return home that her daughter, but nearly six years old, had been rushed to hospital because of internal pains. She was operated upon. Following this, complications set in and but a week or so later the little lass passed away. The sorrowing parents laid her to rest in Lambourne End Churchyard.

Less personal, but moving nevertheless, was the midwifery case she had to attend; illustrative, too, of some of the terrible conditions of the times. This I have recorded on tape and I think I can do no better than to let the tape, with but minor editing, 'speak' for itself.

'This particular night; I remember it so well. It was in September and it was a beautiful evening. A man had come to the door and said: "Would you please come to this address?" I had no idea; the name I did not know. I had not booked the case, and also, the man did not say he was the husband; only the messenger. I said to the man: "This is not my district." He said: "I've been to the doctor; the doctor has gone to London; the doctor's mother said: 'The midwife lives at such and such address. She must go. She is the nearest one to go to this person, as, also, this case has not been booked by the doctor.'"

'So the midwife went — me, of course. My acetylene lamp had been filled. I went out, bonnet and bag and all. I knew not of course where I was going and, unfortunately, I did not take very much notice of the route I took. It seemed a very long way. Well! he said: "This is the place", then disappeared. It was a very low thatched cottage and on a common. I went in and the woman was in absolutely advanced labour. Of course, it was a very long way we cycled and it had apparently taken him a long time to get me.

'I was really horrified. Never in my life had I seen anything like it; never been in a house like it or a cottage. There were two little children in the room where the woman lay. They huddled on the floor on straw and covered up with coats. The woman lay on the bed, with newspapers and rags, but not a mattress; with straw, I suppose, or wheat chaff — what they used to use. There was no fire. The woman had hardly any covering at all. Well! I hadn't time to view the scene as I had other things to occupy my mind and the baby was advancing very quickly.

'I went into the kitchen; the fire — there was just a little wood fire. I couldn't find the kettle. All I could see was a frying pan and a Glaxo tin. There was an old-broken-down table on an all-brick

floor and I hadn't anywhere really to put my bags, or to sort out
anything. Fortunately I'd taken a hand towel, which I always
carried with my soaps and disinfectants and things I required for
the midwifery, for the delivery. But I was stumped for water. So I
said to the woman: "Where do you get your water?" She said: "It's
in a bucket, somewhere." I did see a bucket of water but whether
it was clean or not I could not say. "Well!" I said: "Where's your
kettle?" "Oh! they smashed it up this morning. We haven't got a
kettle; the handle came off." So I said: "What have you got
nearest to a kettle; have you got an old saucepan?" "Oh! that leaks
at the handle; that's broken." So I said: "The nearest thing, then, is
a frying pan."

'So I put a frying pan on just to wash my hands. I had to clean
it the best I could. In the meantime I said: "Is there no one here
who can help?" "Well," she said, "my mother-in-law has just had
a row with me and cleared off." So I said: "What's going to happen
to the children?" "Oh! – they'll be all right. They won't wake up;
they never do." So I said, "Oh! very well. Have you got a bowl?"
"No; there's an old tin there – a Glaxo tin; a large tin." I told her I
would make use of that to wash my hands. I had only got a
frying pan full of water, so I didn't want much of a basin. So I did
the best I could. The Glaxo tin was fairly clean. Well! Then I
carried my own little bowls; used all my disinfectant; put some
more water into the frying pan, which was cleaner, for my bowl
use and then said: "Have you anything in which I can wrap the
baby?" "Oh no! I didn't know I was having the so-and-so kid; I
didn't bother." I told her: "Somebody has got to bother. What's
this, here?" "Oh! it's an old shirt, which I thought might come in."
Whether it was her husband's – this shirt – I didn't know, because
I never did find the husband. He was not available, for some
unknown reason. So I tore up this shirt and made something in
which to wrap the baby when it was born. I said: "You must now
prepare yourself for the birth. I can't look about any longer. We
must do that afterwards."

'Well! things advanced very quickly and the baby was born. All
I hoped and prayed was that the little ones who lay on the floor –
the straw – would not wake up. Well! the cry of the baby of
course disturbed the kiddies. So I managed to get the baby born.

The baby came quite naturally; everything was satisfactory. I then happened to look up to the ceiling, I think, giving thanks to God, that everything was safe, so far. I saw a pair of eyes peering through the cracks in the ceiling — Yes! that is perfectly true. I was really horrified to think that human beings could be so cruel to let a woman lie there alone and hide herself up in another bedroom and look at me and all that was going on below, through this crack in that ceiling. It incensed me very much. I didn't say anything to the woman. I thought she had plenty to get on with. So, just as the baby really gave a good cry, up woke the children. I covered Mother up — the best I could; separated the baby and wrapped it in the shirt I'd made; got hold of the children before I could proceed with anything else, then bundled them into the kitchen.

'So, we proceeded then much more comfortably but, in the meantime, the lamp gave out and as the woman had no candles I had to get out my acetylene lamp (from the cycle), put that on to finish the delivery and attend to other things. I finished the delivery. The acetylene was working quite well. I straightened Mother up the best I could. I had nothing clean whatsoever to put under her. She'd just got some brown paper which was very useful at the time because it kept her bed dry — you see? I managed to put the other part of the old shirt on to the mother, also straightened her up the best I could. I attended to the baby with the Glaxo tin. I'd put that on the stove with water and that heated very nicely. This was an old-fashioned stove with a hob to it, so the tin stood lovely on it. I did the baby's eyes and mouth with my own cottonwool and sterile water which I had in my bag and then proceeded to tidy the baby. I couldn't what you call wash it because I hadn't anything in which to wash it, except sponging it on my lap. There was some kind of towel which I used; I supposed it was a bit of sheet or something; then finished with my own towel which I carried with me. Well! I tidied up everything; put the baby back with its mother; got the children. They said they wanted a drink of water so I gave them a drink and then said: "I think you've got a baby sister. You had better come back to bed and take care of her while I get Mummy something to eat or drink."

'Still this woman didn't appear. I couldn't see her anymore. She'd disappeared from upstairs. At least I didn't see her again. So I boiled some more water in the frying pan; said to the mother: "Have you any milk or food. I could give you a little drink or bread and milk or something?" She said: "I don't know what there is in the house; there was a little jar of Bovril." I said: "That'll do beautifully. Have you any bread?" There were only a few crusts of dry bread on that table. I couldn't see any food anywhere. I didn't know where the cupboards were. I don't think there was any food. The children hadn't any. So I said, "I'll use these crusts up and put them in a cup of Bovril." I made her that. She drunk it and said she felt comfortable and that she would go to sleep. "That's the best thing you can do. Will there be someone here to look after you?" She said: "I don't know whether my mother-in-law will come in now the baby's here." I said: "Where's your husband?" "Oh! he cleared off. I don't know here he is." "Where is the man who came to fetch me?" "He was the man who lived across the green."

'There was no neighbour so I did not know what to do. After making the mother comfortable and putting the children back to bed, I went across the common to inquire if they knew the man who came to fetch me for Mrs So-and-so's baby; and where was the husband? They said they didn't know. I then thought how am I going to get home. I'd never been there before; I didn't know the way; it was half-past twelve at night. No man came back, so the only thing for me to do was to tell the children, as I was going to find Granny and to tell her. The boy was bigger than the girl and he understood. I made him understand. I had also told those people across the green that I was leaving her — going home, if I could find my way. Would they please keep an eye on her until I came in the morning or until the doctor came? There was nothing else to do. "She is perfectly all right but should she be be taken ill you must ring the doctor, so-and-so." I gave the doctor's number. I said, "It's no use coming for me. He's got a car. He can get there much quicker than I, should there be an emergency."

'So I went back to the woman and told her: "Now you make sure; your mother is here somewhere but she will probably come after I've gone and if anything unforeseen turns up, get in touch with the doctor you went to in the first place. Whether it's your husband or the messenger across the green, I don't mind who it is as long as you get in touch with your doctor; if not, get in touch with the policeman; one or the other."

'Well, I said goodnight to them; had another last look – temperatures, pulses, baby – everything. All were correct and I proceeded to go home. I'd no food. I had had a very early tea but I didn't stay to have an evening meal at home. It was now going on for one o'clock. My acetylene lamp was just a flicker when I started out. It had burnt out in the meantime and I had no more acetylene to replenish it. I had no light.

'All I had was the tall trees, the hedge, which I remember passing, by a wood – a rough wood. It started to rain. I hadn't a mac; only a cloak – a serge cloak. It had been a beautiful night and I never thought to put on a mac – and – I didn't realize it was so far. I had no idea where I was going along the road and it was so out of the way I didn't see any cottages; and it was one in the morning. Had I done so I would have been terrified of waking up anyone at that time in the morning. They might have thought I was breaking in or something so I just kept looking at the fir trees, looking at the road and it was pouring with rain. I just kept on walking. I walked round, only to come back to where I had started. Round the wood I went but didn't come to a main road. Apparently I should have turned off somewhere in that area, which at first I didn't do.

'Eventually, I saw a cottage, which must have been about three in the morning. Dawn was just beginning – it was a light dawn, so I could see more. I went to the cottage and a man came to the window. "My God!" he said, "You're miles from where you want to go. You want to go right down there, Missus; turn left and then right." That's what I should have done in the first place – you see! But of course I didn't.

'Well! I didn't mind because the grey light – the dawn – began to come. The water was dripping out of my bottom; all out of my clothes. I got on my bicycle; I didn't mind that and I cycled along, maybe then about seven or eight miles from my home. It was probably more than that because I had a long way to go before I could get to the main road, because I was right out of my area.

At last I got home — my husband's sister was staying with us, looking after the children, and they were terribly worried. My sister-in-law had said to them: "Auntie will want a bathe when she comes home, so I'll put a copper of water on." I must say we had no bathroom. We had a cottage bath, and she put on that copper of hot water.

'So I arrived home; dripping wet. It was still pouring with rain. I should think it was just on six o'clock. I'd been travelling all that time, walking and riding the best I could in the dark. I'd had no food. I just stood on the doormat. My husband was a-bed. Auntie had stayed up because she was worried. You see, I said I would not be long. I stripped off my clothes, right off just where I stood. She took hot water straight from that copper and put it into the bath. I got into this bath; put in some mustard to take off the chill and gave myself a good mustard bath.

'The next morning I'd lost my voice but I had to get up to go to the doctor. Well! eventually I telephoned him and was able to tell him what had happened. He said: "I'm very sorry, nurse, you take the responsibility of this case, therefore you must continue to do it as a midwife." I told him I had no idea where it was. "You'll find it in the daylight." So I had to take the responsibility. I couldn't break any rules. I had to go.

'Fortunately I hadn't anything very important at the time, so I got on my bicycle and asked my way; groped my way back to this woman. On the way there I called at the house of a patient I knew had got some baby clothes and I borrowed, begged and stole these baby things to put the baby in. I went to some other lady and got some bedding for the woman, also a night-dress; sheets, too, for the bed.

'In all that time I never met the husband. I had to go to that case for the then specified time of ten days; each day. Fortunately, I hadn't another baby case, only general work. I went for ten days, and the funny part — or shall I say the artful part, — I thought I would never get any money — fees — from this woman. So one day — one morning — I met the insurance agent, who was going to pay this woman two guineas. "Well!" I said, "that is my money; which belongs to the Nursing Association." He said: "Very well, nurse; you've earned it. You shall have it."

'I got the two guineas. The woman-did very well and the baby – there was nothing wrong with it; nothing wrong with the woman. She was as strong as a horse; a good thing for her and me that she was so.'

Time marched on. In 1929 the Barretts marched on too – to Norfolk. Anne the nurse, no longer – Sister Barrett was the designation, thus proving that experience, as ever, played its part. Holt and the surrounding area were to be for several years more very familiar to her as she travelled on her rounds tending the sick and bringing innumerable babies into the world and the arms of the grateful mothers.

Came the Second World War and the official retirement of Sister Barrett. No retirement from nursing, however, because demands were still to be made on her skills and the next few years brought more moves within Norfolk to satisfy those demands of others for her to continue in the realms of private nursing. Her final 'case' brought her to Framingham Pigot. In course of time even the demands of this last patient were halted and at long last calls for her skills from the outside world seemed to have been brought to a close.

It was of course impossible for Anne to turn her back on nursing, because she had yet one more patient on which to ply her crafts and skills – her own husband. We know of her devoted attention to him. From this time there was a steady deterioration in W. H.'s health. The strain of constant attention was having its effect on Anne too; not surprising bearing in mind that some eighty-two summers had passed her.

So the weeks went on. Anne strove hard; drove herself hard too. By this time W. H. was often oblivious to the happenings around him. In appearance he had changed as a result of a full-blossomed white beard; looked as like a patriarch as one could imagine. Later, quoting from my diary 'Went to Mr. and Mrs. Barrett's. He's in a poor way – helped Mrs. to feed him. He is 83 – cannot communicate or recognize anyone.' On 15 October, W. H., on the danger list, was taken to hospital. Tenaciously the old Fen Tiger clung on to that ever-weakening thread of life; for over two weeks. It snapped, as we know, on Saturday, 2 November 1974.

Many letters of sympathy reached Anne from, as she told them, 'my babies'; mature folk now who are scattered not only in widely separated places in this country but from faraway overseas places too. The sorrow, sadness and heartache which descended on her are now slowly but surely lifting through the agency of yet another nurse — Time. Someone once said: Live as though you are going to die tomorrow; plan as though you are going to live for ever. Possibly Anne agrees with the sentiment of the first part. Of a certainty she endorses the second, judging from her expressed plans for future activities.

Meanwhile, there is just one more patient on which the life-long nurse keeps an ever-watching eye — that of her own good self — because of the unwelcome attentions of that non-discriminator of persons, arthritis. Of one thing one can be certain, any struggle will not be given up lightly by Anne. The nurse, who has, in addition to her own strong character and optimistic outlook, through nearer sixty than fifty years' association, the against-adversity-fighting strain of the old Fen Tiger, whose pen, alas! roves the paper no more.